Finance and World Order

Recent Titles in
Contributions in Economics and Economic History

American Trade Policy, 1923–1995
Edward S. Kaplan

Bastard Keynesianism: The Evolution of Economic Thinking and
Policymaking since World War II
Lynn Turgeon

Latin America in the World-Economy
Roberto Patricio Korzeniewicz and William C. Smith, editors

Information Technology as Business History: Issues in the History
and Management of Computers
James W. Cortada

Dollars Through the Doors: A Pre-1930 History of Bank Marketing in America
Richard N. Germain

The Intellectual Legacy of Thorstein Veblen: Unresolved Issues
Rick Tilman

Inequality: Radical Institutionalist Views on Race, Gender, Class, and Nation
William M. Dugger, editor

Mass Production, the Stock Market Crash, and the Great Depression:
The Macroeconomics of Electrification
Bernard C. Beaudreau

The Logic of Privatization: The Case of Telecommunications in the Southern
Cone of Latin America
Walter T. Molano

The Dilemmas of Laissez-Faire Population Policy in Capitalist Societies:
When the Invisible Hand Controls Reproduction
Marc Linder

A Tramp Shipping Dynasty—Burrell & Son of Glasgow, 1850–1939:
A History of Ownership, Finance, and Profit
R. A. Cage

The Economic Basis of Peace: Linkages Between Economic Growth and
International Growth
William H. Mott IV

Finance and World Order

Financial Fragility, Systemic Risk,
and Transnational Regimes

Adriano Lucatelli

Contributions in Economics and Economic History,
Number 186

GREENWOOD PRESS
Westport, Connecticut • London

Library of Congress Cataloging-in-Publication Data

Lucatelli, Adriano, 1966–
    Finance and world order : financial fragility, systemic risk, and
transnational regimes / by Adriano Lucatelli.
        p.   cm. — (Contributions in economics and economic history,
    ISSN 0084–9235 ; no. 186)
    Includes bibliographical references and index.
    ISBN 0–313–30378–9 (alk. paper)
    1. International finance.   2. International economic relations—
History.   I. Title.   II. Series.
HG3881.L72   1997
332′.042—DC21   96–47432

British Library Cataloguing in Publication Data is available.

Library of Congress Catalog Card Number: 96–47432
ISBN: 0–313–30378–9
ISSN: 0084–9235

First published in 1997

Greenwood Press, 88 Post Road West, Westport, CT 06881
An imprint of Greenwood Publishing Group, Inc.

Printed in the United States of America

The paper used in this book complies with the
Permanent Paper Standard issued by the National
Information Standards Organization (Z39.48–1984).

10 9 8 7 6 5 4 3 2 1

To Christiane

Contents

Tables and Figures

TABLES

FIGURES

Preface

Since the breakdown of the Bretton Woods system in the early 1970s the relationship between states and markets has undergone a tremendous transformation. Deregulation, the abolition of exchange controls, and technological advances have increased the power of transnational finance at the expense of the states. The voluntary retreat of states has cleared the field for nonstate actors and thus helped create a truly global single market for the provision of financial services.

These developments coincided with the renaissance of liberal thinking in the Western world. With the internationalization of private finance the liberal paradigm that has always advocated the free interaction of market forces and a minimal role for the state saw its full realization. Recently however, liberal doctrine has come under great pressure. The argument is that the wave of deregulation of financial markets has brought new risks. Interventionists claim that most of the crises in the financial services sector since deregulation have had their origins in the imprudent behavior of financial players in the "unregulated" marketplace. As financial intermediaries become increasingly involved in international transactions, they hold that it has become virtually impossible for national authorities to monitor the safety and soundness of the financial services industry. The only effective response for the interventionists would be a reversal of the deregulatory initiatives or at least higher cooperation among national authorities.

These arguments echo the ideas of some economic historians who maintain that a departure from the liberal paradigm is necessary for social order and stability (Polanyi, 1944). This book does not, however, lend any support to the idea that state intervention is a prerequisite for overcoming the supposedly destabilizing forces of a self-regulating market system. Therefore, it does not follow that the public regulatory environment has to be strengthened globally to prevent a financial crisis. In fact, it is not at all obvious why many economists refuse to entertain the possibility that deliberately created transnational institutions play a vital role in maintaining order and stability in global finance. First, many financial intermediaries have created a compliance officer function that reduces financial fragility by supporting the different business units and helping the bank to comply with existing rules and regulations, including advising on the structuring and engineering of financial transactions. Second and more important, financial intermediaries have established procedures, norms, and rules that help prevent systemic risks.

Against this background, this book advocates the transnational regime theory, which provides an instrument for conceptualizing the internationalization of private finance and directing attention to a new way of structuring the international environment. It also advances a policy prescription for helping maintain order and stability in the global financial market.

ACKNOWLEDGMENTS

Many people helped me develop the above arguments, and it is therefore a great pleasure to record my deep gratitude. I would like to thank Dieter Ruloff, director of the Swiss Institute of International Studies at Zurich, who showed great interest in this theoretical debate and helped me formulate my ideas more precisely. Among those who read and commented on the manuscript in whole or part, I will be especially obliged to Ulrich. I was also lucky to have the invaluable help of Andrea, Carmen, Christiane, Norine, Phillip, Rachael, Vasili, and Vjeko for the final preparation of the manuscript. They have not only brought order to my chaos of drafts, but also contributed a great deal to the literacy of my manuscript. Moreover, I should record my thanks to the librarians of Credit Suisse and the Swiss National Bank whose assistance saved me a great deal of time.

Introduction

Throughout the history of the modern state system, which was legally created by the Peace of Westphalia in 1648, there have been two fundamentally opposed schools of thought: (1) the Hobbesian or realist tradition (Hobbes, 1651) and (2) the Kantian or cosmopolitanist tradition (Kant, 1784, 1795). Realists hold that the key actors in world politics are states that are driven by the quest for power and assert that they act to benefit themselves at others' expense. Due to the absence of an overarching authority, states are therefore left with the uneasy task of accumulating instruments of physical violence to solve the problem of national security. This also requires that economic activity be subservient to the states' interest in power. As a result, world order and stability are merely achieved through the balance of power.[1]

The Kantian school of thought, on the other hand, projects an optimistic worldview. The central reality of world politics for cosmopolitanists is not the system of states, but the community of humankind. In contrast to realism, the Kantian approach does not assume international relations to be a distributive game, but argues that there is essentially a harmony of interests. Cross-border economic activities are a source of peaceful relations among societies because international trade produces mutual benefits. Thus, it is the cosmopolitanist society that stands in the focus of interest.[2]

---

1. Order is here defined as a system of rules and procedures governing the behavior of all actors, whereas stability is understood as a condition in which these rules and procedures are firmly established and not easily changed by the actors.

2. For an outline of the various forms of cosmopolitanism, see Lucatelli (1994).

Despite their valuable insights for the study of international order and stability, the two perspectives nonetheless display some deficiencies. For example, the assumptions of the realist thinking have the effect of rendering nonstate actors not only epiphenomenal, but invisible and mute, and thus fail to acknowledge that order is achieved by nonstate agents as well. Second, they exaggerate the inhibitory effects of the anarchic structure toward cooperation. The Kantian paradigm, on the other hand, makes the liberal mistake of playing down the obstacles to world order while correctly underscoring the relevance of nonstate actors for the maintenance thereof.

These deficiencies were shown up by the internationalization of financial services and markets. Since the late 1950s, barriers that once insulated domestic markets from foreign competition have been dismantled and modern electronics and other ground-breaking technologies have facilitated the establishment of a global communications and trading system. This created a huge playground (*Casino Capitalism*, Strange, 1986) for financial intermediaries, enabling them to become not only global players but independent agents of change. Yet, the liberalization of financial markets has also brought new risks. For instance, global turnover in the major foreign exchange market segments amounted to an estimated daily average of $1.2 trillion, which poses enormous settlement and systemic risks. In fact, if one party were to declare its insolvency the whole system could come under great pressure. Paradoxically, the voluntary retreat by states from the global financial market thus produced incentives for competiton *and* cooperation. In order to manage cross-border financial relations efficiently and effectively financial intermediaries have therefore had to come up with their own cooperative institutions (procedures, norms, and rules). Against this backdrop, it is theoretically and empirically deceptive to ignore the emergence of nonstate actors and their arrangements. Accordingly, it becomes most important to incorporate the cosmopolitanist ontologies into a single study of world order. Yet this book does not seek to come up with a general theory. By following the trail pioneered by other transnationalists (Deutsch, 1957; Haas, 1958, 1964; Ruggie, 1975), it will advocate a new theoretical form of the cosmopolitanist approach by the provision of a rational footing: *the theory of transnational regimes.*[1]

This book will hence advocate a "middle" way that lies between the imminent threat of interstate anarchy and the utopia of a world government. It will supply an in-depth examination of nonstate actors and their transnational regimes. It will

---

1. Borrowing from Krasner's concept of international regimes (Krasner, 1983), transnational regimes can accordingly be defined as institutions (principles, norms, rules) that regulate transnational actions within a particular issue-area. It is worthwhile noting that transnational regime theory makes the distinction among principles (beliefs of fact), norms (standards of behavior), and rules (prescriptions for action).

show that the transnational perspective offers a promising way to study world order in an era that is characterized by the simultaneous appearance of both international and transnational actors. In order to support this argument, it will test ("falsify") transnational regime theory by applying it to an important arena of action: the global financial market. With the help of case histories, it will analyze the contributions of financial intermediaries[1] to the maintenance of world order and stability in the light of the management of state insolvency after 1982 through the London Club and the establishment of private netting arrangements for the direct settlement of global foreign exchange deals. In so doing, this study obviously endorses the top-down approach (i.e., deduction) and therefore departs from induction. Rather than involving one single method for the process of discovery and the logic of validation (i.e., observation, generalization, testing), it advocates the deductive way to knowledge, which subjects theories emerging from human thinking and its resultant hypotheses to logical testing. Experience here is thus not the building block of theory but its touchstone.

Case history analysis is a most valuable approach to transnational relations. It provides the opportunity to develop a rich understanding of conditions, processes, and outcomes that have governed the emergence of transnational institutions, and as such, offers a tool for testing the implications of the proposed theory as well as developing thinking about global affairs. In fact, by tracing the establishment and maintenance of transnational institutions, this book not only supports the theory of transnational regimes, but also directs attention to a new way of providing order and stability in the global financial marketplace. In the absence of a global authority checking on the global activities of financial intermediaries, transnational regimes become a viable option for areas that states have voluntarily retreated from, such as foreign exchange markets or cross-border payments systems. There is also a lack of mathematical formalism, which is not, however, adventitious. Systems of social order are too complex to be reduced to a rigorous formal model. In spite of its rejection of the formalist orthodoxy, this work does nonetheless emphasize theoretical conceptions, thus owing greatly to the Austrian School (Menger, 1883; Mises, 1949; Hayek, 1978) that professes a non-formal *but* deductive approach.

In terms of methodology, this study aspires to positivism. True, all social scientific theories involve a certain element of interpretation. Facts of history are never perfectly objective because historical objectivity stands between fact and interpretation (Carr, 1961). Thus, only in its most deterministic version could social scientific theory ever be subjected to a rigorous testing along the lines of Ayer or

---

1. Transnational financial intermediaries are here defined as actors that both own and control financial activities in two or more countries. These are universal banks, commercial banks, and securities houses.

Lipsey (Ayer, 1936; Lipsey, 1963), let alone to testing along the lines of Popper or Lakatos (Popper, 1935; Lakatos, 1980). Nonetheless, the emphasis is on experience (observation and testing) as the only possible way to justify claims to knowledge about the social world.

In summary, then, the following chapters will:

- explain the original formulations of transnational regime theory;

- offer a comprehensive account of how financial intermediaries came to prominence in global affairs;

- evaluate how financial intermediaries contribute to world order and stability; and

- provide a policy prescription for authorities to include transnational regimes in the global regulatory system.

1

Transnational Regime Theory

Sempre la pratica dev'essere edificata sopra la bona teorica.

—Leonardo da Vinci

Even though the state is still a dominant actor in international relations, it has undergone a tremendous process of transformation. The state has become more and more penetrated by nonstate actors that challenge its control over territory and sovereignty.[1] Nowadays it is no longer unusual that, at times, nonstate actors wield great power over states through their transnational activities or through their ability to circumvent state control. These developments obviously have changed the structure of the global system, resulting in "a profusion of systemic ties, whether power dominated or legitimized, extending over a variety of functional dimensions and involving a range of actors at and between various levels, which create world, regional, local and territorial ties" (Groom and Heraclides, 1985: 175).

Keohane and Nye were among the first to attempt to conceptualize this transformation of the international system (Keohane and Nye, 1973, 1977, 1989). They

---

1. It is common to distinguish among subnational, transnational, and supranational actors. Subnational actors are entities that are capable of bypassing the machinery of the home state. Transnational actors are entities that have foreign branches that do business in other countries or that are socially, politically, or religiously active in various foreign countries. Supranational actors are bodies that transcend national limits by confining the sovereignty of member states.

realized that, given the emergence of new actors that all have distinct interests and stages of activity, it is no longer feasible to take the unrestricted dominance of the state for granted. Unfortunately, their analysis was incomplete. Remaining realists by conviction, they were unwilling to accept the fundamental implications of their outlined transnational approach. As Kegley and Wittkopf correctly argue, "a careful reading of *Power and Interdependence* indicates . . . that the transnational relations and interdependence paradigm does not reject realism" (Kegley and Wittkopf, 1989: 26). This criticism is not, however, intended to dismiss the useful works of Keohane and Nye, but rather to highlight a particular gap in their study that the present book aims to address.

The argument in favor of nonstate (and particularly transnational) actors fits neatly into the concept of neoliberalism (or ordoliberalism, as it is called in Germany). When the major liberal assumptions about the state, economy, and society can be reduced to only one denominator, then it is a firm defense for the free development of the individual (Eucken, 1939, 1952). This does not, however, deny the importance of institutions. Rather, ordoliberalism provides for behavioral conventions that emerge from the bottom up and usually arise without any organizing authority. These conventions help coordinate interaction and achieve increased safety, more convenience, higher productivity, or lower transaction costs. For classical liberals, this is even more true for the international than the domestic realm.

Accordingly, this study maintains that it is necessary to formulate a systemic, transactional perspective that includes nonstate actors and that takes into account the contributions of transnational actors in maintaining world order by establishing transnational regimes. In light of the emerging global system, which is characterized by the simultaneous appearance of both state and nonstate actors, this book therefore makes the case for transnational regime theory.[1] The similarity with earlier forms of the transnational perspective is by no means adventitious. Rather, this work seeks to follow the path created by other transnational theorists (Deutsch, 1957; Haas, 1958, 1964; Ruggie, 1975). Furthermore, it owes a great deal to the insights of the neoliberal (or neorealist) concept. Transnational regime theory involves the rational choice assumptions for reasons of parsimony just like neo-

---

1. Transnational regime theory is very much like Locke's (1689) social contract theory, arguing that in order to enjoy the benefits of a cooperative society individuals in a state of nature voluntarily surrender their rights (see also De Jasay, 1989: 40–69). Transnational regime theory also has roots in the Hayekian philosophy of an (intrinsically voluntary) spontaneous order in a market environment (Hayek, 1944, 1983). Unlike the Hayekian concept, transnational regime theory does not, however, fail to distinguish conceptually between spontaneous order and the enforcing order that institutionalizes the behavioral conventions of the spontaneous order.

Table 1.1
Comparison between Transnational Regime Theory and Neoliberal Institutionalism

	Transnational Regime Theory	Neoliberal Institutionalism
Actors	Unitary-rational firms	Unitary-rational states
Motivations	World order and stability	World order and stability
Processes	Transnational cooperation	Interstate cooperation
Outcome	Rule-governed behavior through the creation of transnational institutions	Rule-governed behavior through the creation of international institutions
Regimes/Institutions	Advisory committees; netting schemes; International Securities Market Association (ISMA); etc.	Intergovernmental organizations; international regimes; international conventions; etc.
Independent variables	Transnational regimes can act as independent variables	Interstate institutions can act as independent variables
Definitions of regimes	Institutions (principles, norms, rules) that regulate transnational actions within a particular issue-area	Institutions with explicit rules, agreed upon by governments, that pertain to particular sets of issues in international relations (Keohane, 1989: 4) Principles, norms, rules, decision-making procedures around which actor expectations converge in a given issue-area (Krasner, 1983: 1) Multinational agreements among states which aim to regulate national actions within an issue-area insofar as they define the range of permissible state action by outlining explicit injunctions (Haggard and Simmons, 1987: 495)

liberal institutionalism, and thus differs only insofar as it focuses on the role of nonstate actors, whereas neoliberalism stresses cooperation among states (see Table 1.1). Against this background, transnational regime theory should be understood as an analogy drawn from the neoliberal (or neorealist) paradigm.

ORIGINAL FORMULATIONS OF TRANSNATIONAL REGIME THEORY

Transnational regime theory starts with the assumption that nonstate actors together with states are among the most important players in the international political economy. Borrowing from economics, it also assumes that nonstate actors are unitary-rational agents, meaning that transnational actors make choices guided by self-interest. Furthermore, it implies that rational agents order their possibilities consistently; thus, if Actor A prefers X to Y, and Y to Z, consistency requires that Actor A prefer X to Z. Consequently, rationality contains two branches: self-interest (broadly defined) and consistency (narrowly defined). In addition, transnational regime theory concedes that the market system considerably stifles the actors' willingness to help overcome potential market failures. It, however, neither devalues the probability for cooperation nor belittles the potential of formal or informal transnational institutions. That is, even though the market is considered as being anarchical in the sense of lacking central decision-making institutions, which thus makes it difficult to provide for public goods, the transnational paradigm firmly believes that nonstate actors can establish institutions that intervene by altering the incentives to produce public goods. The argument goes that transnational regime theory does not equate system only with structure, but holds that systems possess two dimensions: structure and process. It thus synthesizes both structure and process into a system-level theory (Table 1.2). In keeping with the liberal tradition, transnational regime theory argues that regimes are a human construct and, once created, have effects of their own on people's thoughts and actions.

In essence, the arguments of transnational regime theory are twofold: (1) institutions/regimes are relevant and (2) the determinants of institutions can be analyzed through the methods of economics. Thus, it goes beyond neoclassical microtheory, which takes institutions for granted and treats them as things that lie beyond theory and do not need to be explained. As Eggertsson nicely says:

microeconomics, in its conventional form, treats organizations and institutions the same way as it treats the law of gravity: These factors are implicitly assumed to exist but appear neither as independent nor as dependent variables in the models. Such economy in model making can be eminently reasonable. It enables us to isolate critical relationships and simplifies the use of mathematical tools in the analysis. However, unlike the law of gravity, organizations and institutions are not invariant. . . . Once [the] research questions involve variable organizations and institutions, either as exogenous or endogenous variables, conventional microeconomic analysis becomes a rather blunt instrument. (Eggertsson, 1990: xi)

Table 1.2
Original Formulations of Transnational Regime Theory

Actors	Unitary-rational nonstate actors that are transnationally active
Structure	Important force shaping actor preferences and choices
Processes	Management of problems
Outcome	Rule-governed behavior through the creation of specific forms of transnational cooperation
Institution	Independent force facilitating transnational cooperation

In order to develop its key assumptions about transnational cooperation, transnational regime theory starts from the market idea—or the "invisible hand," Adam Smith's marvelous metaphor of the market system (1776). However, it argues that markets, at times, undersupply public goods and thus create market failures. In such situations actors find themselves in positions that can be illustrated by the game of prisoner's dilemma (Axelrod and Keohane, 1986).[1] In this game, each actor has an incentive to defect regardless of whether the other party cooperates or defects. For example, if the second party cooperates, the first party prefers to defect (DC>CC). But if the second party defects, the first party still favors defection (DD>CD). The dilemma emerges because, if both defect, they will be worse off than if they had cooperated (CC>DD). Accordingly, DC>CC>DD>CD.

Yet prisoner's dilemma does not advance the notion that defection is preferable to cooperation or that parties should defect when mutually favorable outcomes are possible through cooperation. It simply demonstrates the structural attributes of situations in which parties follow a course that logically leads to an outcome that is not Pareto-optimal. Transnational regime theory now affirms that counterforces exist to resolve the prisoner's dilemma. It employs this game to demonstrate that parties may have interests that are simultaneously competing and cooperative. Instead of each party realizing a gain that is equivalent to the other's loss, both parties can do better or worse.

In essence, there are three sets of conditions that favor transnational cooperation under competition. First, prisoner's dilemma can be modified into a less conflictual game by altering the payoff structure such that the order of preference for both

---

1. Moral philosophy claims to have found a way of circumventing this dilemma without breaking out of the confines of a rationality in which the decisions are only made for the reason of maximizing the expected payoffs of each of the players (Gauthier, 1985).

parties becomes CC>DC>DD>CD. In other words, by increasing the benefits from joint action compared to those arising from defection, the "dilemma" can be overcome. Second, transnational cooperation is more likely to emerge if the game is repeated indefinitely (the so-called iterated prisoner's dilemma) rather than if it were played only once. When both parties know that the game will continue and that the payoff structure will not be changed decisively by a particular game, they will realize that the benefits from joint action exceed those from other outcomes (Axelrod and Keohane, 1986: 232). As Axelrod argues, "enlarging the shadow of the future" facilitates cooperation among self-interested parties (Axelrod, 1984: 129). Third, cooperation can be encouraged by reducing the number of actors. The presence of only a few actors makes it much easier to identify and achieve common interests or to negotiate agreements. As Keohane says, "contemporary international relations are beset by dilemmas of collective action, but these dilemmas are rendered less intractable by the small number of states involved" (Keohane, 1984: 77).

True, the game-theoretic approach reveals some of the conditions under which transnational regimes can arise, but it fails to explain both the organizational form and scope of such regimes. The functional approach remedies this shortcoming by explaining the emergence of regimes in terms of their effects on actors: every regime has a function and the function explains its presence.[1] Functional theory is essentially post hoc in nature; that is, after regimes have been created, their existence is then accounted for by examining the incentives that have confronted nonstate actors that first established and now maintain them. Of course, functional theory cannot predict how or when regimes will be supplied, but it is useful in helping specify when regimes are needed. Nevertheless, the functional argument should be regarded with great caution. Unless a functional analysis can show that a given institutional arrangement is reasonably well adjusted to the interests of the nonstate actors that maintain it, it will fail to make a causal argument. In other words, functional arguments have to establish a sensible causal link between the regime, on the one hand, and its existence, on the other. The biggest risk of functional explanations is, therefore, the fallacy of interpreting the emergence of regimes on the basis of the "functions they must have served, when they in fact appeared for purely adventitious reasons" (Keohane, 1984: 81). By showing that the involved parties are rational and that the regimes, which are to be explained, are designed to fulfill anticipated functions, the fallacy can, however, be circumvented. That is, by assuming that transnational actors have anticipated the effects of their behavior, it is possible to establish a cause–effect relationship, and it is viable to explain the occurrence of transnational regimes by understanding their functions.

---

1. See especially Jensen and Meckling (1976).

Clearly, transnational regime theory has borrowed from neoclassical microtheory with its two distinct characteristics: (1) the unit of analysis is the individual firm, which is regarded as rational; and (2) diverging behavior of the individual is not irrational, but conditioned by the modified parameters influencing the available choices. As Keohane argues,

The key distinguishing characteristic of a systemic theory is that *the internal attributes of actors are given by assumption rather than treated as variables*. Changes in actor behavior, and system outcomes, are explained not on the basis of variation in these actors' characteristics, but on the basis of changes in attributes of the system itself. (Keohane, 1983: 508–9)

In summary, then, the transnational perspective differs from other theories of world politics in relation to actors, dynamics, and dependent variables. Regarding actors, transnational institution theory sees nonstate actors as dominant cast members, though not the only ones. Regarding dynamics, it sees complex transactions between nonstate actors. Regarding dependent variables, it sees the establishment of transnational institutions (e.g., transnational regimes). In regard to the specific concepts (the building blocks), the theory refers to order and transnationalism.

EXPLANATORY POWER AND PARSIMONY

It is only feasible to accept new theories if many different phenomena can be explained, which means that these theories have to be convincing in two respects: explanatory power and parsimony. Because it is cumbersome and extremely difficult (maybe even impossible) to collect all necessary information, parsimony and simple explanations are obviously very helpful in understanding complex social events. On the other hand, theories also need explanatory power to render them useful. Thus, the higher the degree of the two dimensions, the more powerful are theories and the less likely that pure chance accounts for the theories' success. Furthermore, the plausibility of theories depends on their ability to explain not only different aspects of a single phenomenon, but a wide variety of events and facts. Of course, there is always the danger that events and historical facts are chosen selectively to fit the respective theories and that phenomena that might disprove or falsify their explanatory power are suppressed. To counter this risk, it is necessary to incorporate as many facts as possible into a previously defined and delineated category in order not to draw a distorted picture; this way theories can be applied consistently, thus avoiding the risk of applying them discriminately. This book will attempt to do so by referring to the global financial market (i.e., the global credit market and foreign exchange market) to prove the explanatory power of transnational regime theory. Parsimony, on the other hand, also has its limits. Even though theories should be able to explain social events, they can by no means explain everything. A particular theory might be true, but, on the same token, cover only some aspects of social reality.

DEDUCTIVE CRITIQUE OF TRANSNATIONAL REGIME THEORY

The most notable criticism of transnational regime theory concerns "rational-ism." For reasons of both "parsimony" and "predictive capacity," it presumes that all nonstate actors are rational and therefore approach the problem of adapting to the challenges posed by market failures in similar ways. Despite the virtues promised by rational choice, it is obvious that the impediments to seeing actors as unitary-rational agents are substantial; the acceptance of rational assumptions requires a view of rationality that does not exactly reflect processes of human choice. As the *Economist* pointedly says:

Temptation. Fear of getting hurt. Lack of self control. Regret. A desire to be fashionable. Religious belief. Over-confidence. Bad habits. All are part and parcel of everyday economics. Most contemporary economic theories assume that humans are rational, and so tend to ignore apparently irrational behavior. (*Economist*, 24 December 1994: 92)

In fact, subsystemic forces, such as organizational and bureaucratic politics and individual psychology, tend to conflict with coherence and rationality.[1] More important, students of world politics, whom Keohane has called "reflective" (Keohane, 1989), have always argued that rationalistic theories of institutions have no endogenous dynamic.[2] In the words of a "reflective" scholar:

Like all social theories, rational choice directs us to ask some questions and not others, treating the identities and interests of agents as exogenously given and focusing on how the behavior of agents generates outcomes. As such, rationalism offers a fundamentally behavioral conception of both process and institutions: they change behavior but not identities and interests. (Wendt, 1992: 391–92)

In other words, game-theoretic and rational choice analyses neglect the roles of ideas as a source of interest and the issue of institutional learning and thus fail to refer to intersubjective epistemology or ideological structures to explain the emergence of cooperation. It is therefore necessary to supplement the theory of transnational institutions with the insights of a "cognitive" approach. This could be, for instance, the "epistemic communities approach," examining the role that knowledge-based experts play in facilitating the establishment of institutions (see Adler and Haas, 1992; Haas, 1992a, 1992b). It is claimed that new ideas and information, which are diffused by knowledge-based experts, can lead actors to learn new patterns of reasoning or to follow new interests. An example of this could be the Institute of International Finance, whose membership is made up of financial intermediaries and whose primary purpose is to disseminate information to its

---

1. See Allison (1971); Holsti (1970); and Jervis (1976).

2. See also Kratochwil and Ruggie (1986); and Kratochwil (1991). The argument is that the ontology and epistemology in the regime debate are not congruous.

members and to provide a communication forum for the key actors in the international lending process. It might also be such rating agencies as Moody's, Standard and Poor's or IBCA, all of which provide vital information for investors and lenders by analyzing the creditworthiness of companies and financial intermediaries all over the world. Indeed, credit ratings are becoming an increasingly important factor in the global capital market. As global issuers try to raise capital in cross-border markets, investors providing these financial resources are focusing more attention on credit quality before making their final decisions. The rating system is designed to produce an accurate and consistent picture that allows global investors to evaluate and rank risks across industries or countries and types of risks. As Bohn of Moody's says: "In today's financial markets, information is power, but *only* if the information is of the highest quality" (quoted from Moody's, 1991).

The knowledge-based communities approach hence plays an important role in transforming identity and interest. In so doing, it bridges the rational choice and the reflective institutional approaches, thus explaining the source not only of interests but also of institutions. This suggests that transnational regime theory should be supplemented by the insights of the "reflective" approaches. However, an in-depth analysis of the epistemic communities approach would go beyond the scope of this book and shall therefore be left for another study at a later stage.

WHAT MAKES TRANSNATIONAL REGIMES OBSTINATE?

International regime theory is certainly not new, but has a long tradition that goes back to Grotius and Vattel, the "founding fathers" of international law. What is new, however, is the application of the regime approach to the transnational realm. Thus, transnational regime theory, as an offspring of the liberal paradigm circumscribing institutionalized structures (principles, norms, rules, procedures), is a specific form among others; it has to be regarded as an element of an overarching theory of global cooperation. Similar to international regime theory, the transnational approach analyzes and studies the institutionalization of cooperative activities. It also looks at regimes as independent variables and assumes that regimes influence actors.

The biggest challenge to theories on institutions is the proof of their relevance; it is clear that regime theory is only meaningful where actors are influenced by the institutions involved. In the case of transnational regime theory, however, institutions only exist because they are vital in maximizing the private actors' utility.[1]

---

1. This is indeed the biggest difference between interstate and transnational regimes. The transnational approach is basically bottom up. Institutions are not forced on the actors, but evolve. Law enforcement comes about as a result of market mechanisms rather than from a hegemon's decisions.

Accordingly, if these institutions do not perform their jobs *efficiently*, they will disappear.[1] In this market view of transnational institutions, it is unnecessary to study their relevance, because all inefficient institutions will fall victim to the selection process of the Darwinian market, thus fully rejecting the null hypothesis.[2] Consequently, the measurement of the outcome (i.e., goal attainment) and the institutional effect become irrelevant[3]—a fact that is further supported by the focus of rational-choice-based institutionalism on problem solving (Yarbrough and Yarbrough, 1990: 254). All the above factors therefore make it possible to construct detailed narrative accounts (i.e., case histories) that trace causal paths from institutions to outcomes.

POLITICS VERSUS ECONOMICS

On a more general level, this work forms part of the still growing body of scholarship on international political economy that attempts to bridge the gap between politics and economics. It acknowledges the fact that the segmentation has had an inhibitory effect on a thorough understanding of global affairs and therefore attempts to explore the interface between the two fields of study. But why did politics and economics become separated in the first place? According to Polanyi, it was the existence of a self-regulating market, dating back to the eighteenth century, which required the division of social reality into a political realm and an economic realm (Polanyi, 1944). A similar argument has been put forward by Groom and Heraclides, who see the reason in the Industrial and French Revolutions. The former brought into being a world economy and the growth of transnational transactions, whereas the latter was the "harbinger of the nation-state which gradually imposed controls on these transactions" (Groom and Heraclides, 1985: 175). The separation between the two distinct academic subjects is, however, only a century old and dates back to the so-called marginalist revolution of the 1870s. It was Marshall, one of the most dominant scholars in U.S. and British economics in the late nineteenth and early twentieth centuries, who changed the name of the subject single-handedly by arguing that the

nation used to be called "the Body Politic." So long as this phrase was in common use, men thought of the interest of the whole national when they used the word "Political;" and then "Political Economy" served well enough as a name for the Science. But now "political interests" generally mean the interests of only some part or parts of the nation; so that it

---

1. Efficiency means the highest possible ratio of output to input. In such a situation it is not possible anymore to achieve a Pareto improvement by reallocating inputs or outputs.

2. The null hypothesis holds that, ceteris paribus, the goal is attained without the respective institutions.

3. On measuring outcomes and effects of institutions, see also Bernauer (1995: 364–77).

seems best to drop the name "Political Economy," and to speak simply of *Economic Science*, or more shortly, *Economics*. (Quoted from Staley, 1991: 133–34)

Likewise, Morgenthau, a steadfast realist, was also a strong defender of the necessity of separating politics from economics analytically, though for different reasons:

Intellectually, the political realist maintains the autonomy of the political sphere, as the economist, the lawyer, the moralist maintain theirs. . . . It is exactly through such a process of emancipation from other standards of thought, and the development of one appropriate to its subject matter, that economics has developed as an autonomous theory of the economic activity of man. To contribute to a similar development in the field of politics is indeed the purpose of political realism. (Morgenthau, 1973: 13–16)

Over the years, to many observers it seemed, however, that the separation was very unhelpful in understanding international affairs. Some prominent political scientists therefore started to look for ways to overcome this conceptional division by synthesizing politics and economics, though warning that it is not enough to simply say that politics does not take account of economic forces and vice versa (Staniland, 1985; Strange, 1989). So far, only a few have succeeded in formulating a theory that successfully combines politics and economics. Strange maintained that one of the main reasons for this omission has been the tendency to take the other subject for granted. According to her,

Markets are studied in economics on the assumption that they are not going to be disrupted by war, revolution or other civil disorder. Government and the panoply of law and the administration of justice are taken for granted. Politics, meanwhile, assumes that the economy will continue to function reasonably smoothly—whether it is a command economy run according to the decisions of an army of bureaucrats or a market economy reflecting the multiple decisions taken by prudent and profit-maximizing producers and canny consumers. (Strange, 1989: 14–15)

The two different approaches to politics and economics clearly show why it has been perceived to be so difficult to synthesize the two subjects. In order to cut through the artificial divide between the two spheres, it is therefore necessary to enlarge the ontology. This is exactly what transnational regime theory does. By arguing that states have voluntarily retreated from certain political areas to make room for nonstate actors, transnational regime theory embraces an ontology that incorporates elements of both politics and economics. In fact, financial intermediaries have already performed political functions by providing order and stability through transnational institutions, even though they stand in daily competition. The most famous examples are the London Club in the credit market and the netting schemes in the foreign exchange market—both as a result of the internationalization of private finance and the retreating states.

2

The Rise of Private Finance

> Governments have lost the power to control capital, and they have probably
> lost it for ever.
>
> — David C. Roche

Since the end of World War II international investment has not only expanded
exponentially, but also changed dramatically: big enterprises, commonly referred
to as transnational corporations (TNCs), have mushroomed all over the market
economies. Their phenomenal growth has also alarmed national governments as
the prospect of TNCs overwhelming national sovereignty or even overpowering
international economic arrangements has increasingly become a real possibility.
The argument has been that transnational corporations have begun to be a source
of power themselves.

What factors have contributed to the enormous power of TNCs? The most
important has certainly been government policies that have aimed at the liberalization of trade and capital flows. There is also Coase's internalization theory, according
to which a firm is the means of coordinating production without using market
exchange (Coase, 1937). Applied to TNCs, this means that the coordination of
production without using market exchange takes the firm across national boundaries.
In addition, there has been the enormous technological progress in communication,
which reduced the costs of global information as well as the processing of that
information. Finally, there have been territorial advantages, such as low labor and
tax costs as well as fully developed infrastructure that TNCs try to exploit. The
unique properties of TNCs naturally came to challenge the autonomy of states. As

Spero says, they "reinforce[d] the multinational corporations' tendency to make decisions with concern for the firm and the international environment and not with concern for the particular states in which it is operating" (Spero, 1990: 106). This is even more true for transnationally active financial actors. Says Ruloff:

The banks of the global financial market are undoubtedly the most important nongovernmental players in the world: some of these banks are financially stronger than lots of countries, and they are not the only ones—so are some other transnational corporations. Unlike the latter, though, the big banks operating in the global financial market compete directly in some of their activities with government institutions, the central banks, and are successful at it. Why? Because, in contrast to the big transnational corporations, which largely pursue their different kinds of businesses unaffected by each other, the banks operating in the global financial market are extremely well organized among themselves. If absolute mutual trust exists anywhere in an area otherwise marked by dog-eat-dog competition, it is in international currency trading. (Ruloff, 1988: 81)

Clearly, Ruloff's observation suggests that nonstate financial players have become important, active agents of change in international relations. In order to appreciate how financial intermediaries perform alongside states on the global stage, it is necessary to analyze in detail the internationalization of private finance, or, to use Sarver's words, "the process of interlinking financial markets in different countries into a common, worldwide pool of funds to be accessed by borrowers and lenders alike" (Sarver, 1990: 516).[1]

INTERNATIONALIZATION OF PRIVATE FINANCE

Much has been written about the increasing internationalization of economic activity since the end of World War II. The greatest bulk of scholarly attention, however, has focused on the growth of global trade and transnational business. Only recently did academia shift its interest to private international finance. This late honor can be largely explained by the fact that in contrast to the growth of transnational trade and business, the internationalization of private finance was not deliberately planned. Says Hans-Jörg Rudloff, former member of the executive board of CS Holding, "no one forced the creation of this market. It wasn't planned or organized by any government" (Rudloff, 1993: 193). How, then, did private finance become an influential agent of change?

In the late 1940s and early 1950s, private finance on a global scale was virtually nonexistent. Financial flows across borders were regulated and directed by both governments and international public institutions, while national markets had been separated from each other due to inconvertibility of national currencies and strin-

---

1. For an econometric measurement of global money market interrelationships, see Lin and Swanson (1993).

gent capital controls. It was only in the late 1950s that private financial intermediaries tentatively began to move abroad. Yet rather than borrowing and lending in
and out of the highly regulated domestic markets, financial intermediaries were
operating in the so-called offshore Euromarkets,[1] which function outside any
government control such as capital adequacy standards or interest ceilings and thus
exist in a void (i.e., this money is not included in the national monetary base), so
to speak. Surely, this form was neither envisaged nor foreseen by the founding
fathers of the postwar international monetary order, which may explain why the
Articles of Agreement of the International Monetary Fund (IMF) paid little attention to short-term capital movements or to international private capital transaction
of any kind of qualification.

The internationalization of private finance continued at breathtaking speed
during the three following decades. Its development, however, differed significantly from that of the 1950s. National financial markets began to integrate, and,
in so doing, made direct borrowing and lending between domestic markets much
easier. Hurdles for movements in and out of the offshore markets were slowly but
surely removed. Moreover, Euromarkets were geographically reaching out, thereby
incorporating markets outside the North Atlantic region (Helleiner, 1989: 3). By
the early 1990s, the internationalization process was eventually completed through
the removal of the last remaining barriers between offshore markets and domestic
markets, on the one hand, and between different national markets, on the other. The
distinction between international and national markets virtually disappeared and
the geographic outreach reached its fullest extent, thus making the financial markets
truly global in scale. In sum, then, the internationalization of private finance can
conceptually be divided into three phases: (1) 1950–early 1960s; (2) 1960s–1970s;
and (3) 1980s–1990s.

Interestingly enough, Maynard Keynes and Harry Dexter White had repeatedly
warned of such a scenario. Keynes stressed that

It is widely held that control of capital movements, both inward and outward, should be a
permanent feature of the postwar system—at least so far as [the position of the British
government] is concerned. If control is to be effective, it probably involves the *machinery*
of exchange control for *all* transactions, even though a general open license is given to all
remittances in respect of current trade. But such control will be more difficult to work,
especially in the absence of postal censorship, by unilateral action than if movements of
capital can be controlled *at both ends*. (Horsefield, 1969: 13)

---

1. The origin of the term "Euromarket" can be traced back to the French Banque
Commerciale pour l'Europe du Nord, in which the former Soviet Union chose to place its
large stocks of dollars and which was better known by its telex code "EUROBANK." The
term "Eurocurrency" means money deposited by corporations and national governments in
banks away from their home countries, called "Eurobanks."

Likewise, supporting tough restrictions on short-term capital movements, Harry Dexter White's blueprint (the so-called White Plan) proposed the following:

Each country agrees (a) not to accept or permit deposits or investments from any member except with the permission of that country and (b) to make available to the government of any member country at its request all property in form of deposits, investments, securities, of the nationals of member countries, under such terms and conditions as will not impose an unreasonable burden on the country of whom the request is made. (ibid.: 66)

The reason for this was

Its acceptance would go a long way toward solving one of the very troublesome problems in international economic relations, and would remove one of the most potent disturbing factors of monetary stability. Flights of capital, motivated either by prospect of speculative exchange gains, or desire to avoid inflation, or evade taxes or influence legislation, frequently take place especially during disturbed periods. Almost every country, at one time or another, exercises control over the inflow and outflow of investments, but without the cooperation of other countries such control is difficult, expensive, and subject to considerable evasion. It would seem to be an important step in the direction of world stability if a member government could obtain the full cooperation of other member governments in the control of capital flows. . . . The search for speculative exchange gains or desire to evade the impact of new taxes or burdens of social legislation have been one of the chief causes of foreign exchange disturbances. (ibid.: 66–67)

Despite these warnings, the internationalization of private finance was proceeding at an imposing speed and went about making worldwide nets, woven tightly together by SWIFT, CHIPS, GLOBEX, and Reuters and Telerate.[1] Many explanations for this postwar phenomenon have been put forward, the most common being theories that stress the importance of technological revolution[2] or that emphasize economic necessity.[3] However, a closer look immediately reveals that they do not

---

1. SWIFT means "Society for Worldwide Interbank Financial Telecommunications." It was founded in 1973 to cope with the large increase in global payments. It is an electronic payment system located in Brussels, Belgium. CHIPS stands for "Clearing House Interbank Payments System," the international private clearing system in New York City for Euromarket transactions. It is an electronic payment system operated by the New York Clearing House Association. As of the end of 1990, it had 131 participants. GLOBEX is the latest automated global transaction system of the Chicago Mercantile Exchange (CME), Reuters, MATIF (Marché à Terme International de France), and DTB (Deutsche Terminbörse), which allows for round-the-clock futures and options trading. Reuters and Telerate are wire market information services.

2. See Huertas (1990: 263) for the argument that technology was a fundamental force in globalization in banking.

3. As early as in the 1950s, Robinson (1952) maintained that financial development followed economic development, though only in a domestic context. More recently, Ruloff argued that international investment was the major driving force behind the globalization of private finance (Ruloff, 1988: 79–80).

hold much water. First, technological innovations accompanied and accelerated an already ongoing process. Second, it does not follow that cross-border trade necessarily depended on financial intermediaries rather than the two public Bretton Woods institutions, the IMF and the International Bank for Reconstruction and Development (IBRD, known as the World Bank). Challenging the explanatory power of the two theories, Helleiner correctly comments that they fail to explain why the process took place in "such an odd combination" of different stages and why the geography changed through each of the stages. Moreover, these theories fail to show why globalization took place "via the segmented euromarkets initially and then change[d] to more direct integration" (Helleiner, 1989: 4). As Helleiner suggests,[1] any attempt to answer these questions will end up with the observation that it was the policies of states that directly or indirectly promoted the internationalization of private finance through liberalizing policies so as not to bear the painful costs of adjustment to structural changes in the world economy (Helleiner, 1994).[2] This argument was elaborated by Alan Greenspan at the International Monetary Conference in June 1994 in London, where he stated that the global integration of financial markets has been a product of public decisions (*Neue Zürcher Zeitung*, 9 June 1994).

Early Growth Period

There were basically three groups that supported the growth of transnational financial actors: the United Kingdom, continental Europe, and the United States. Of the three parties, Britain was the most strident defender of the formation of Euromarkets for several reasons. Most important, both the Bank of England and the City dreamed the daring dream of restoring the stature London had held in the nineteenth and early twentieth centuries. However, the British government, which refused to make sterling freely convertible, openly opposed their endeavors. The bad memories of the failed 1947 attempt at making the currency convertible were still very much alive at 10 Downing Street.[3] Thus, the Bank of England prohibited British banks from engaging in pound financing of third country trade, which was perfectly understandable given Britain's balance-of-payments crisis. By supporting the formation of the Euromarket in London, the government could, however, kill two birds with one stone: it did not have to lessen the stringent regulatory

---

1. For other state-centric explanations of the opening of financial markets, see Pauly (1988); and Underhill (1991).

2. For a policy-oriented analysis of international financing and the problems of adjustment, see Bird (1985).

3. At that time the British economy was still in dismal shape. When the sterling became convertible on 15 July 1947, capital flight immediately ensued, thus depleting the official reserves of Britain.

Figure 2.1
The Growth of the Eurocurrency Markets (U.S. $ billion)

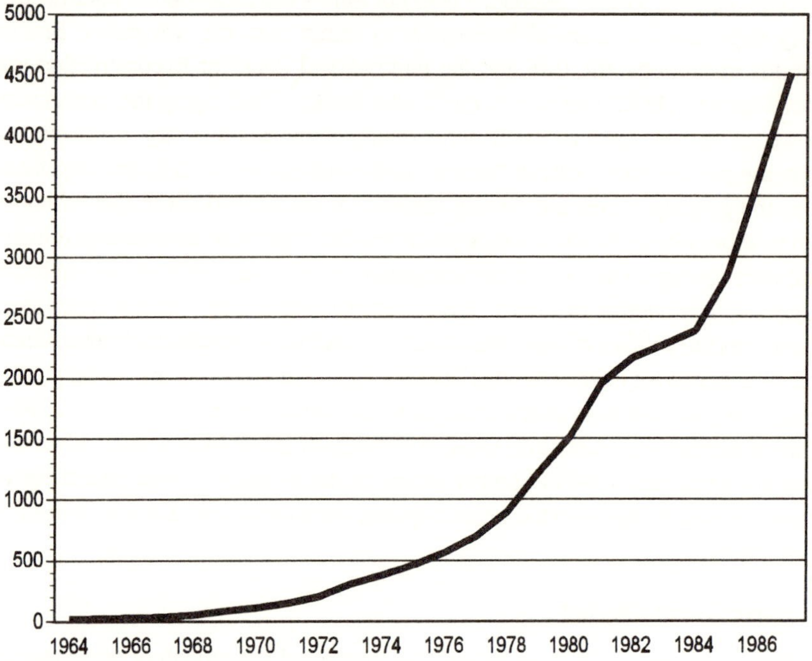

Note: Data based on Morgan Guaranty Trust.

atmosphere and London could be rebuilt as a major financial center. Indeed, the international financial operations of the City were based on U.S. dollars and thus segmented from the national economy.

The United States had a different reason for supporting the formation of offshore centers. It was running a huge external deficit during the 1950s in its attempt to foster the reconstruction of Western Europe and Japan via direct investments by U.S. TNCs and foreign loans provided by U.S. financial intermediaries, and to contain Soviet influence via the North Atlantic Treaty Organization (NATO).[1] As recovery in Europe got under way in the 1960s, the question of who should carry the burden of the adjustment of the U.S. external deficit emerged. According to U.S. business forces, there were basically two ways to reduce the deficit: domestic deflation or cancellation of the U.S. military commitments overseas. But for the U.S. government both responses were out of the question for obvious reasons. It did not want to stifle the U.S. economy, nor did it wish to undermine the Atlantic alliance. Thus, by 1963 U.S. authorities tried to bring the deficit under control by

---

1. From 1946 to 1958, U.S. aid and loans to Europe reached net $25 billion.

imposing stringent restrictions on capital outflows. First, it introduced the Interest Equalization Tax (IET)[1] to discourage foreign bond issues in New York (1963–73) by evening out U.S. and European yields on bonds and stocks, followed by the Voluntary Foreign Credit Restraint Program (1965–73), the Foreign Direct Investment regulations (1965), and the Mandatory Foreign Investment Program (1968–73), which placed limits on loans to foreign clients and investments abroad. Furthermore, U.S. authorities put into effect Regulation Q, which prohibited interest payments on demand deposits and authorized the Federal Reserve to set a ceiling up to which interest was allowed to be paid on savings and time deposits in U.S. banks. Another factor was the legal lending limit, which restricted a financial intermediary's total exposure to a single client to 10 percent of its capital. The losers of these measures were American TNCs and financial intermediaries, which stood to lose their overseas businesses as the right of moving dollars in and out of the United States was being repealed. Again, it was the Euromarkets that helped solve this predicament (Figure 2.1).[2] Since dollar transactions in Europe did not affect the U.S. balance of payments adversely, the U.S. government saw the Euromarkets as a way to rescue the overseas businesses of American enterprises.

Yet the U.S. business community was not the only one that bore the costs of financing the mammoth U.S. external deficit. On the contrary, the Europeans had much to lose from America's growing deficit, which was further accentuated by the Great Society social programs of the Johnson administration and the Vietnam War. Surplus countries such as Germany and Switzerland felt increasing inflationary pressure on their domestic money supply because they had to hold excessive dollars as reserve currency (see Figure 2.2).[3] In order to prevent a further deterioration of their export competitiveness, hard-currency countries took tough measures to counterbalance the upward pressures. Germany, for instance, imposed a Bardepot 40 percent cash deposit on foreign borrowing by German companies, while Switzerland introduced a negative interest rate on nonresident Swiss franc deposits. As the United States still did not show any willingness to control its deficit,

---

1. Securities of emerging markets, international institutions, and Canada were exempt from this tax.

2. The Eurobond market, which was a result of the many U.S. regulatory factors, was initiated in July 1963 by Autostrade, an operator of toll motorways in Italy. The bond had as its lead manager S. G. Warburg and as co-managers several banks from all over Europe.

3. Under the rules of the IMF, established at the Bretton Woods Conference, exchange rates were fixed at a par value in relation to the dollar and fluctuations around this value were confined to a +/- one percent band. Central banks were thus forced to buy (sell) dollars when the dollar reached the lower (higher) intervention point of the band. From this it follows that when the United States pursued inflationary monetary policies, the other countries were compelled either to revalue their national currencies or to let their domestic prices increase. For more details, see De Grauwe (1990: 37–39).

Figure 2.2
Official Reserves, Year End* (SDR billion)

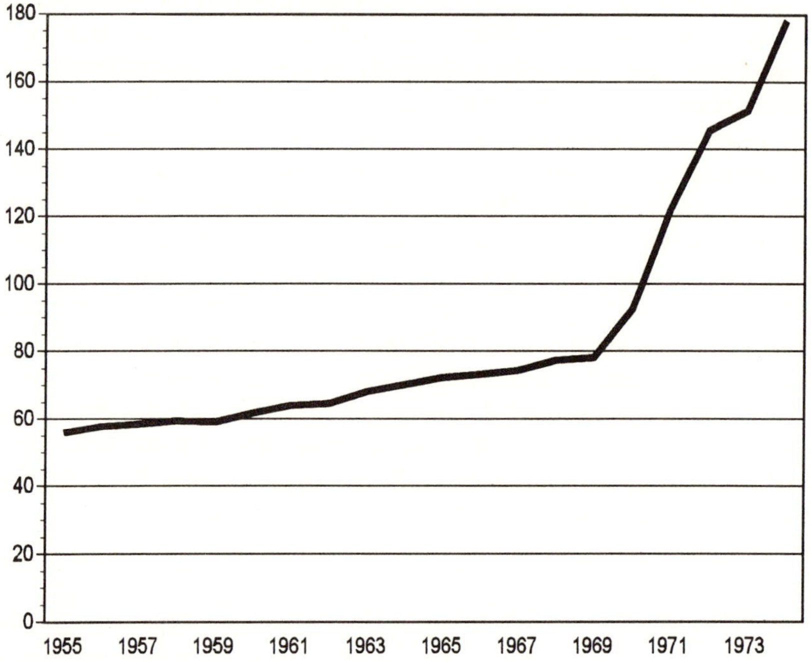

Note: Date based on IMF.

* Official reserves of IMF members and Switzerland

Europeans increasingly resented the self-interested behavior of the United States which enjoyed its position as the world's banker, and its ability to determine the growth of international liquidity through its balance-of-payments deficits.[1] The Euromarkets, however, helped diffuse the inevitable clash between the United States and Europeans. By placing their foreign reserves in more competitive Euromarkets, the Europeans were able to offset the inflationary effect and receive a higher interest rate[2] as well.

Of course, other factors contributed to the formation of Euromarkets, although they were neither necessary nor sufficient. For example, there was the reestablished

---

1. In this context, President Charles De Gaulle of France spoke of the "exorbitant privilege," which meant that the United States was able to invest abroad with its own currency.

2. At that time, "prime + compensating balances" were more than "3/6-month LIBOR [London Interbank Offer Rate] + spread." This was due to the prime-based cartelization and "reinforced by its geographical delineation of markets, fewer new entries, and provision of free services for good corporate customers" (Sarver, 1990: 37).

confidence in the safety of cross-border financial transactions in the 1950s and the desire of financial intermediaries to control balance sheet risk through interest rate swaps and other financial swap agreements. Another factor was the signing of the Treaty of Rome in 1957, which established the European Economic Community (EEC) and gave U.S. corporations the incentive either to buy European enterprises with dollars or to spend dollars in order to establish foreign subsidiaries in Europe. The placement of its dollar holdings in Europe by the former Soviet Union also fostered the formation of Euromarkets. Out of fear that the United States might freeze or even seize their bank deposits, the Soviet Union and its satellites followed the advice of their British merchant bankers by transferring dollar holdings to European banks.[1] Coincidentally, this proposal also fit perfectly with the Soviet strategy of increasing relations with Western European countries. In a similar position were some Arab investors. They feared that their U.S. dollar holdings in New York could be frozen just as Egypt's assets were during the Suez War of 1956. In this case, the United States froze the assets of all belligerent actors when it learned about the Franco-British-led invasion to recapture the nationalized Suez Canal and about the Israeli plan to destroy terrorist hideouts without prior notification. This was obviously enough incentive for Arab investors to transfer their holdings out of the United States. Finally, there was the Italian input toward the growth of Euromarkets. Financial intermediaries in Italy were initially restricted in lending lira due to a fixed lending rate structure. By bidding for U.S. dollar deposits to make corporate loans in U.S. dollars, they could, however, circumvent restrictions in lira interest rates.

Late Growth Period

By the early 1970s, the strains caused by the U.S. external deficit had become so heavy that the rules of Bretton Woods were in need of revision. In 1971, President Nixon suspended the convertibility of foreign central banks' dollar reserves into gold, thus throwing the monetary system into disarray. The weakened system was eventually abandoned two years later, when foreign exchange rates were left to float freely. In addition to the large U.S. balance-of-payments deficits, there was the 1973 oil crisis. The Organization of Petroleum Exporting Countries (OPEC) succeeded in quadrupling world energy prices, thus dealing another blow to the system. Because of the severe impact of the oil crisis on international balances of payments governments were once again forced to realign their national currencies. True, the postwar monetary system could have been prevented from collapsing if the participating countries had cooperated. Yet unsurpassable disagreements

---

1. In fact, important events such as the coup d'état in the former Czechoslovakia, the Chinese civil war, the Berlin blockade, the Korean War, the Rosenberg trial, and the notorious McCarthy hearings aroused anti-communist sentiment at this time.

among the United States and the European countries thwarted a powerful public response. The reason was that the Euromarkets turned out to be a welcome window of opportunity.[1] They allowed the parties to postpone the painful adjustments that a multilateral rescue attempt would certainly have entailed. Thus, it was the unwillingness of the parties to bear the costs of adjustment that was responsible for the sudden rapid growth as well as the beginning of the geographical spread in the early 1970s.

This begs another question: exactly what was the United States to gain from the formation of Euromarkets in the 1970s? By supporting the internationalization of private finance, the United States could continue to follow its unilateral expansionary course without having to fear external constraints on domestic policy, at least not until the 1978 dollar crisis.[2] In fact, Euromarkets freed the United States from any adjustment pressures and so allowed it to retain full policy autonomy. As regards the Europeans and Japan, the reasons for promoting the privatization of international finance were also to be found in the desire to postpone the necessary adjustments to global structural changes. That is, the rise in the oil price led to giant imbalances in the international payment system that could only be handled less painfully if they were financed (Pecchioli, 1983: 26–33). Yet the IMF had already lent so much money that public financing was not available. This was the moment when transnational banks stepped in and helped out by recycling the so-called petrodollars. Of course, the deficit countries could have adopted measures of fiscal and monetary deflation. But in the 1970s governments were aiming at mitigating rather than aggravating the fall in real income. In order to finance their imbalances governments began to borrow from Euromarkets and to liberalize their domestic markets. The British-based economist Panic states that

loan financing became much more important than bond financing. Up to 1973 eurocurrency credits featured less prominently in international capital markets than external bonds. For instance, between 1970 and 1972 their average share of the market was only 39 percent. The relative importance of the two forms of finance fluctuated a good deal over the following six years (1973–78), but eurocurrency credits became considerably more important, accounting, on average, for 57 percent of the total. Their share increased further after 1979, to 67 percent or more. (Panic, 1988: 247)

Thus, it was essentially the opening of domestic markets to promote capital inflows or outflows that was most vital to the integration of national markets.

---

1. Between 1972 and 1981, the external lending of banks in the member states of the IMF rose at an average annual growth rate of 26 percent, that is, from $264 billion to $2,138 billion (Köhler, 1992: 6–7).

2. Monetary expansion in the United States in 1976–77 caused a sharp depreciation of the dollar in 1977–78, forcing the Carter administration to follow a restrictive monetary policy.

Table 2.1
Financial Innovation and Liberalization in Europe

United Kingdom		Italy	
1979	Abolition of exchange controls	1978	Creation of unlisted securities market (USM)
1980	Creation of unlisted securities market (USM)	1983	Lifting of credit controls
1982	Opening of the London International Financial Futures Exchange (LIFFE) and London Traded Options Market (LTOM)	1984	Creation of mutual funds
1985	Introduction of interest-bearing current accounts	1987	Securities market reform program
1986	Big Bang (stock market reform)	1990	Last phase of abolition of exchange controls

Germany		France	
1986	Creation of bond options market	1979	Introduction of Fonds Communs de Placement mutual funds
1987	Opening of the unlisted securities market (USM)	1983	Creation of unlisted securities market (USM)
1988	Introduction of the DAX stock index	1984	Abolition of credit controls
1989	Securities distribution system outside official trading hours	1985/86	Issuance of negotiable credit instruments
1989	Introduction of stop-loss and stop-buy orders	1987	Creation of stock options market
1990	Creation of the Deutsche Terminbörse (DTB)	1988	Opening of the Marché à Terme International de France (MATIF) options market
1991	Introduction of the inter-banking information system (IBIS)	1990	Last phase of abolition of exchange controls

Note: Data based on OECD.

Consolidation

The 1980s were characterized by the process of "competitive" deregulation and the enormous development of highly sophisticated financial products.[1] In the United States it was mainly the Depository Institution Deregulation and Monetary Control Act (DIDMCA) of 1980, the establishment of International Banking Facilities (IBFs) in 1981, and the 1982 Garn-St. Germain Depository Institution Act that substantially liberalized the U.S. financial market. Most attention certainly focussed on the introduction of the International Banking Facilities. They were first proposed in the late 1960s in response to the Voluntary Foreign Credit Restraint Program passed to restrict U.S. banks from increasing their lending abroad and thus to control the U.S. balance of payments. IBFs were then viewed as a way to circumvent these restrictions without negatively affecting the balance of payments. However, out of fear that IBFs would curtail its autonomy in domestic monetary policy, the Fed successfully opposed their introduction until the 1980s.

The most significant advantage of IBFs is the lack of any reserve requirements and Federal Deposit Insurance Corporation (FDIC) deposit insurance. Another advantage is that IBFs are exempt from both state and local taxation as long as they are funded from abroad. Despite the many benefits they offer, IBFs have never been in a position to compete equally in the Euromarket. One of the reasons is that IBFs are not allowed to lend to or accept deposits from U.S. residents. This means, for instance, that if the parent borrowed funds from its IBF, it would have to pay the required reserves on Eurocurrency borrowing. This limitation on business with U.S. residents is extended even further by the obligation of IBFs to accept only deposits related to foreign operations. Another important handicap is that IBFs are subject to U.S. laws that prevent them from introducing bank secrecy laws.

At the same time, in Europe it was the "Big Bang" in Great Britain and the "Petite Bang" in France that had deregulated their respective equity and debt markets (Table 2.1). Whereas France, given its statist stance, was cautious in deregulating its financial market, the United Kingdom proceeded with great enthusiasm, not the least due to the traditional hands-off policy of the Bank of England. In October 1986, the Financial Services Bill was put into effect to continue the path of financial deregulation. Stockbroker and market maker functions were merged, minimum commissions were abolished, and the stock exchange and the International Securities Regulatory Organization were merged into the International Stock Exchange (ISE). France, on the other hand, contented itself with small steps, such as the introduction of the Marché à Terme International de France (MATIF) in 1986, the futures exchange, and the abolition of capital controls in light of the European Single Market in January 1990. Equally important for the global integration of

---

1. For an assessment of the financial innovation, see Mayer (1986).

Table 2.2
Chronology of Major Events of the Deregulation Process in Tokyo, 1984–94

June 1984	Trading in government bonds
April 1985	Deregulation of interest rates on money market certificates (MNCs) of 50 million yen or more with maturity one to six months
June 1985	Secondary market for certificates of deposit (CDs)
October 1985	Decontrol of interest rates on deposits of one billion yen or more with maturity between three and twenty-four months
February 1986	Entry of foreign members to the Tokyo Stock Exchange (TSE)
February 1986	Creation of short-term money market
December 1986	Opening of the Japan Offshore Market (JOM)
November 1987	Expansion of the market for commercial papers for Japanese corporations
September 1988	Trading of stock index futures in Tokyo and Osaka
June 1989	Decontrol of interest rates on small money market certificates of three million yen or more
May 1990	Introduction of options on government bond futures by TSE
August 1992	Bond issuance restrictions eased: more companies are allowed to issue bonds overseas and restraints on "Samurai" bonds relaxed
September 1994	Removal of controls on ordinary-deposit interest rates and some other instruments

Note: Data based on *International Currency Review*, Takeda and Turner (1992).

national financial markets was the development of new financial products such as derivatives. Increased competition among transnational banks has forced them to come up with ever more complicated and tailor-made instruments to enhance their market shares.

The most important factors that contributed to the ongoing globalization process in the 1980s were, however, the policies of Japan and the United States, which both saw Euromarkets as a means of weakening the heavy impact of adjustment.

Table 2.3
U.S. Budget and Trade Deficits, 1979-84

	Budget Deficit	Trade Deficit
1979	$40 billion	$28 billion
1980	$74 billion	$24 billion
1981	$79 billion	$27 billion
1982	$128 billion	$32 billion
1983	$208 billion	$58 billion
1984	$185 billion	$108 billion

Note: Data based on U.S. Department of Commerce.

Explaining the reason for lifting the barriers separating Japan from the global monetary and financial system, Helleiner says:

Through the 1950s and 1960s, Japan had promoted high savings in order to supply a large source of funds for corporate investment and growth. When growth slowed down in the early 1970s and corporate demand for funds decreased, savings rates remained high and thus a surplus of savings emerged. Throughout the 1970s, these savings were absorbed by expanding government deficits. But in the late 1970s, there was growing political resistance to the expanding government deficits, led by the Ministry of Finance (who feared a departure from the postwar norm of balanced budgets) and big business (who worried that future taxes would fall largely on them). In the face of the failure of the attempt to expand the tax base in 1979, this group began to successfully push for cut-backs in government. . . . The side-effect of this political movement was that the excess savings were no longer being absorbed.[1] (Helleiner, 1989: 10)

The only way to divert the threat of recession was to find profitable investments for these savings. By placing the surplus in the United States, where interest rates were higher, Japan found the needed investment outlets. Financial deregulation was therefore aimed at facilitating the recycling of Japan's surplus savings (Table 2.2).

The year 1984 was arguably the most significant milestone in the history of Japanese finance; it marked the beginning of a wide range of liberalization

---

1. Fiscal deficits in Japan became daily business with the flotation of government bonds to cover postwar deficits in 1966 and the tremendous growth in deficit in 1971. The immediate impact of the failed expansion of the tax base in 1979 has been the decline in official debt from a total of 14.4 trillion yen to a total of 13.8 trillion yen (Sakakibara, 1984: 167).

measures, such as the United States–Japan accord. As a result of the bilateral talks between the Japanese finance minister and the U.S. Treasury secretary in 1983, Japan promised to take all the necessary steps to integrate its financial market into the OECD region, including (1) the internationalization of the yen; (2) the strengthening of the yen; and (3) the deregulation of capital and financial markets. Japan also agreed to form together with the United States the so-called Yen/Dollar Committee, with the goal of investigating possible further measures to deregulate the Japanese market.[1] U.S. pressure on Japan was certainly heavy, but contrary to popular belief, the pace of the financial deregulation in Japan would not have been so rapid and far-reaching had Japan's problems not been compatible with those of Washington. Using Marxist language, Gilpin describes this congruity between the two countries as follows: "[u]nwilling to make the needed domestic reforms, Japanese capitalism . . . required a 'colony' to rid itself of these financial surpluses. The Japanese found this 'vent for surplus' in an America experimenting with Reaganomics" (Gilpin, 1987: 330). Unquestionably, the opening of Japan's financial markets has been as much a product of economic necessity as of U.S. pressure on the Japanese government.[2]

What was the reason for the compatibility of the United States and Japan? The transition from the Carter administration to the Reagan administration in the early 1980s was accompanied by the adoption of a more expansionary fiscal and a more deflationary monetary policy, which ultimately resulted in a huge budget and trade deficit, respectively (Table 2.3). These unilateral policies would have normally entailed adjustment problems had it not been for international private finance. It was in fact largely Japan's surplus savings that financed a big share of the U.S. current account and budget deficits. Since the early 1980s, Japan has thus been a key purchaser of U.S. Treasury bonds and notes. As Gilpin says, "during the Reagan administration the Japanese began to underwrite the American defence buildup and domestic prosperity. Japanese capital flows to the United States have tripled, from an annual rate of $20 billion in 1982 to $60 billion in 1987" (Gilpin, 1990: 18). In sum, then, it was the unwillingness of both the United States and Japan to adjust their policies that gave another impetus to the internationalization of private finance in the 1980s. Through the channels of the world financial system the savings of Japan were placed in the United States, thus enabling Japan to divert the dangers of recession (at that time, approximately 15 percent of Japanese jobs were directly linked to exports), on the one hand, and allowing the United States to retain its policy autonomy, on the other.

---

1. The Yen/Dollar Committee was dissolved in April 1988, after the United States and Japan concluded that the main objectives had been largely achieved.

2. For an analysis of the increased internationalization of the yen, see Tavlas and Ozeki (1991, 1992).

With the gradual integration of Japan, the trend toward deregulation and the liberalization of capital flows definitively gathered momentum. As the Bank for International Settlements (BIS) noted:

By the early 1990s none of the larger industrial countries retained ceilings or other major constraints on lending. Compulsory portfolio investment requirements for banks were rare and, where they existed, of little significance; portfolio restrictions on institutional investors such as pension funds and insurance companies had been relaxed in several countries. Compulsory reserve requirements had been generally reduced. Controls on foreign exchange transactions and international capital flows had largely been lifted. (Quoted from Walter, 1993: 206)

Even though the globalization of private finance has come to a close end with the opening of the Japanese financial market by the 1990s, it has not yet been concluded. The next step involves the incorporation of the DAEs[1] (Singapore, Hong Kong, South Korea, Taiwan) into the global financial market. As the DAEs are not a homogenous group and have different historical experiences, this process will not show a uniform development. The major reason is that Singapore and Hong Kong have already highly developed financial markets and form part of the globalized financial system. Their headstart can mainly be explained by their membership in the British Commonwealth and the fact that the only viable development strategy for city-states had been the establishment of a competitive international banking center.

This does not hold true for South Korea and Taiwan. They are not yet as closely integrated into global financial markets and the number of their tradable instruments is still very limited. The rather late beginning of deregulation in Taiwan and South Korea lies in the fact that the two DAEs would regard the financial sector not as a source of innovation but as a tool to economic development controlled by the authorities. The number of banks and other financial actors thus remained limited and their activities tightly regulated. It was only after the emergence of huge current account surpluses, putting great pressures on them to adjust to new patterns, that both governments began to open their financial markets to foreign intermediaries. They realized that their economies had entered new phases of economic development and that the previous, albeit successful, patterns of development had to be modified. Illustrating this new reality, Lindner says about South Korea:

The large increase in Korea's external position, combined with a relatively inflexible exchange rate, led to very large increases in foreign currency assets held by the Bank of Korea between 1986 and 1989. The increase in Korea's foreign exchange reserves over the four-year period amounted to about 175 percent of the reserve money stock at the end of 1985. (Lindner, 1992: 13)

---

1. DAE stands for Dynamic Asian Economies and refers to the four Asian tigers or the newly industrialized countries (NICs).

The two DAEs were therefore prompted to widen the profitable outlets of investment at home and abroad to avoid "homemade" inflation. Even though markets have not yet adapted to the new role of South Korea and Taiwan as emerging overseas investors, they have nonetheless been remarkably liberalized, as the recent growth of the so-called dragon bond[1] issues nicely shows.

Most recently, the so-called emerging markets have been in the focus of the international interest.[2] True, they are still young and only partially free, but most of them have already launched liberal policies. For instance, Argentina, Brazil, Malaysia, Pakistan, Peru, and Turkey allow foreigners virtually unrestricted access to their stock markets and allow free repatriations of income and capital. Some countries, such as Bangladesh, Chile, Sri Lanka, Thailand, and Venezuela, allow fairly free access with some strings attached as regards to repatriation. In countries such as China, Poland, and the Czech Republic, securities markets have emerged where none existed before. In Africa, some countries have lifted exchange rate controls, liberalized cross-border trade, and privatized state-owned companies. These emerging African countries have realized that for economic growth it is important to free their financial markets carefully.[3] Nonetheless, even though many African countries have made great progress in liberalizing their markets, their endeavors often experience a quick death due to the lack of democracy. In Nigeria, for instance, the army has revoked most of the country's economic reforms and reintroduced foreign exchange controls. Those and other upsets, therefore, suggest that it might still take some time before African economies will be fully integrated in the global financial market.

Even though the process of financial deregulation and liberalization has spread all over the globe, the degree of financial integration still differs in the various regions. For instance, Europe is highly integrated, not the least due to the steps toward monetary union agreed upon at Maastricht. The Japanese financial market, on the other hand, is still much regulated, and it was only in November 1996, when

---

1. Dragon bonds are issues that are listed in Asia and that contribute to the growth of Asian capital markets. The birth of the dragon market can be dated back to the $300 million issue by the Asian Development Bank in October 1991.

2. According to the International Finance Corporation (1995), emerging markets are characterized by a functioning stock market and a per capita income of less than $8,626 (1993). Of course, this definition cuts through the analytical and conceptional division between the DAEs and the emerging markets, and so it comes naturally that the two youngest dragons, Taiwan and Korea, do not only belong to the DAEs, but by way of their early development also top the list of the emerging markets.

3. Economic theory provides good reason to believe in deregulating domestic financial markets to promote economic development. See Andersen (1993: 67–91); De Gregorio and Guidotti (1992); and Pagano (1993: 612–22).

the government of Ryutaro Hashimoto announced its intention to launch a "Japanese Big Bang" by the year 2001—similar to "May Day" in the United States in 1975 or the British Big Bang in 1986—aimed at opening up the country's financial markets, including broadening competition, deregulating asset-related transactions, and rethinking the role of the government in the financial system. Finally, the emerging markets are only now slowly but surely being integrated into the global financial market.

Financial Intermediaries: The New Kids on the Block

The globalization of private finance (Figure 2.3) was mainly the result of explicit or tacit policies of states unwilling to bear the costs of domestic adjustments that allowed transnational financial actors to come to global prominence. This opening was reflected by international lending and the internationalization of securities markets (Eurobonds, Euronotes, cross-border trades in equities). As Underhill says, it was not simply a result of "rational choice leading to greater efficiency for capital formation in the global economy." Rather, the formation of these markets was "part and parcel of political decision and non-decision making by states and other actors—either domestically or within the framework of responsible international organizations" (Underhill, 1993: 5).

While in the 1960s transnational financial actors were essentially passively adapting to external pressures, by the early 1990s they had become key agents of change influencing their environment. This has led Wrinston, one of the most illustrious bankers, to conclude that the globalization of private finance has created a new system—the information system:

Money only goes where it is wanted, and only stays where it is well treated, and once you tie the world together with telecommunications and information, the ball game is over. It's a new world, and the fact is, the information standard is more draconian than any gold standard. They think the gold standard was tough. All you had to do on the gold standard was renounce it; we proved that. You cannot renounce the information standard, and it is exerting a discipline on the countries of the world, which they all hate. For the first time in history, the politicians can't stop it. It's beyond the political control of the world. (Quoted in Frieden, 1987: 114–15)

Even though Wrinston's statement is ontologically misleading, it would none-theless be mistaken to draw from this the conclusion that the role of financial intermediaries is not important. Theoretically, states do have the power to establish tight controls over capital movements, but practically they may not have the capacity to prevent international capital movements. Or, in Bryant's words, "recap-turing lost autonomy might well be like trying to squeeze toothpaste back into the tube" (Bryant, 1987: 156). And even if it were feasible to control funds movements effectively, a responsible government would hardly endorse such a course given the high opportunity costs involved. As Ruloff correctly says:

Figure 2.3
The Globalization of Private Finance

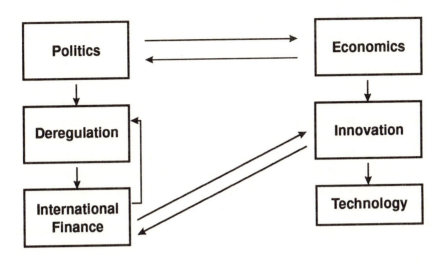

Without a doubt, the Western industrialized countries would be able to dry out the global financial market if they really wanted to. . . . But action that individual countries might very conceivably take against the practices of domestic banks in currency trading would hardly make sense, because the market is flexible enough to thwart it without much trouble. (Ruloff, 1988: 81–82)

In sum, transnational actors in global finance are here to stay. Refusing to accept this fundamental reality would be foolhardy. The likelihood that the *haute finance* could successfully thwart any official attempts at curbing their freedom of actions has to be regarded as very high, as the United Kingdom experienced in 1976 when the government was forced to drop its expansionary policies by the subsequent capital flight.[1] Likewise, the French government had to give up its expansionary fiscal policy in 1982–83 because of international financial pressures.

PRIVATE FINANCE AND WORLD ORDER

Even though states voluntarily retreated from the global financial system, they continued to be ill disposed toward private finance. In fact, ever since financial

---

1. A restrictive climate concerning international private finance would lead not only to capital flight, but to huge market losses all over the world (*Neue Zürcher Zeitung*, 15 November 1993).

intermediaries have been forming transnational networks, authorities have warned of three dangers lurking behind international banking activities: insolvency, illiquidity, and risky foreign exchange operations and positions.[1] So it came that in the wake of the collapse of Herstatt Bank in Germany, the Franklin National Bank in New York, and the British-Israeli Bank in London, all in 1974, the Basle-based BIS launched several initiatives (see Appendix 2), some of which eventually led to the establishment of the Standing Committee on Banking Regulations and Supervisory Practices (the Cooke Committee). It provided not only an informal forum for central bankers and regulators to discuss current issues concerning international banking, but set up precise rules to manage the responsibility for banking supervision (the 1975 Basle Concordat). Aimed at improving supervision of international banking activities, the Basle Concordat was revised in 1983 (as a reaction to the Banco Ambrosiano crisis), and capital adequacy standards for transnational financial actors were set up by the Cooke Committee in 1987 (as a result of the stock market crash).[2]

Since the BIS regime is regarded as weak (Helleiner, 1992) and central bankers have yet to agree on a specific agenda for action (Pecchioli, 1983), officials and scholars alike have been calling for better and more efficient regulatory measures.[3] Indeed, the argument goes that individual banks do not have any incentives to reduce or evade so-called negative externalities (costs that are created by banks in insolvency without compensating the society as a whole) and that therefore government intervention is necessary. For example, before the New York State Bankers' Association on 30 January 1986, Gerald Corrigan, president of the Federal Reserve Bank of New York, said that recent

events have undercut the effectiveness of many elements of the supervisory and regulatory apparatus historically surrounding banking and finance. If it can't be done onshore, it's done offshore; if it can't be done on the balance sheet, it's done off the balance sheet; and if it can't be done with a traditional instrument, it's done with a new one. . . . We must recognize that the historic regulatory/supervisory apparatus associated with banking—whatever its limitations—was a source of restraint and discipline on individual institutions and on the system as a whole. If, therefore, I am correct in postulating that events are undermining that

---

1. Using a somewhat different semantics, Dale distinguishes among foreign exchange risk, the interbank market risk, and country risk (Dale, 1984: 73–89), while Pecchioli differentiates among currency risk, country risk, and maturity transformation risk (Pecchioli, 1983: 138–62).

2. For a comprehensive account of the formation of the BIS regime, see Spero (1980); Cooke (1990); and Kapstein (1989, 1991, 1992).

3. For an overview of the debate concerning the type and scope of regulation, see Portes and Swoboda (1987). See also Dale and Mattione (1983); Dale (1984, 1990, 1992); Lissakers (1984); Pecchioli (1987); Seldon (1988); Gibson (1989); Fingleton (1992); *International Currency Review* (1992); and Herring and Litan (1995).

source of restraint, a key question that arises is what, if anything, should replace it? (Quoted in Dale, 1986: xi)

This should not be the last cry for handcuffs being put on financial intermediaries; it was in fact only recently that these warnings have been dragged up. At the annual symposium of the Federal Reserve Bank of Kansas City in 1993, many participants mourned the weakened influence of central banks over their respective financial markets due to innovation and deregulation. Likewise, public opinion called for tougher public oversight on derivatives after Barings collapsed into administration on 26 February 1995.[1] In doing so, the public feels itself supported by high-profile economists who believe that financial markets are endogenously prone to crises[2] and that consequently an international financial crisis is about to occur when proper institutions do not exist to prevent it. This begs an important question: does the lack of far-reaching and comprehensive public regulation on a global scale mean that international financial crises[3] are inevitable from time to time?

As will be shown in the following pages, transnational financial players are very much able to provide for stable financial arrangements. By forming either ad hoc or preventive transnational regimes, they can help public authorities in performing the role of a lender of last resort (LLR)[4] in emergency cases.[5] Yet, in contrast to states that strive for power and cooperate only if it serves their own interests, financial intermediaries are driven by profit considerations and only collaborate to

---

1. Nick Leeson, a derivatives trader in the bank's Singapore office, bought futures contracts on Japan's Nikkei-225 stock market average and lost over £700 million. It is, however, questionable that public regulation would have prevented the Barings bank from going bankrupt. In fact, the bank lacked an independent risk management unit to check traders.

2. See Goodhart (1988); Guttentag and Herring (1983); Minsky (1982); and Schwartz (1986).

3. Until now, there is still no generally agreed upon definition of a financial crisis. For instance, the participants in the colloquium "Financial Crisis and the Lender of Last Resort," held in Bad Homburg in May 1979, had to admit their failure to come up with a precise definition. As Kindleberger and Laffargue concluded, "a financial crisis is like a pretty girl, difficult to define but recognizable when seen" (Kindleberger and Laffargue, 1982: 2). Of course, a financial crisis has many features, but there is nonetheless widespread agreement that a financial crisis is characterized by a sudden, unexpected, intense demand for money that thus threatens the financial and economic system. See also the Appendix 1 for a more detailed outline of some of the economic theories of financial crises.

4. Discussions of the role of an LLR go back to Thornton (1802) and Bagehot (1873). The argument is that the LLR would provide additional liquidity when a crisis occurs.

5. A private clearing house can indeed act as a lender of last resort as was the case under the American Nation Banking System before the foundation of the Federal Reserve.

contribute to a stable environment for their business activities. From this it follows that interstate cooperation is based on power considerations, whereas transnational financial cooperation is formed for purely profit-seeking reasons. But the same way as interstate cooperation provides for order so does transnational cooperation; that is, by establishing institutions to safeguard their profits, financial intermediaries contribute to the maintenance of world order.

Against this background, the whole debate on the internationalization of private finance and the ongoing controversy about the increased systemic fragility make a superb starting point for approaching and assessing the transnational paradigm. First, the issue brings to the forefront the question of which units (state versus nonstate actors) to analyze in the international political economy. Second, it lends itself as an empirical touchstone against which to test the transnational approach. Finally, in light of the focus of institutionalism on problem solving, it directs attention on transnational regimes as an easy and efficient answer to the management problems in global finance. In fact, as transnational regimes are bottom up and flexible to operate, they offer a way around the problem of national sovereignty.

3

The London Club

Good bankers, like good tea, can only be appreciated when they are in hot water.

—Jaffar Hussein

For a proper understanding of the origins of the debt buildup, it is necessary to analyze the difficulties the IMF encountered in providing ample international liquidity after 1973. That is to say, in the wake of the collapse of the postwar monetary system, the role of the IMF changed considerably; its regulatory role became less important (due to free-floating exchange rates), while its financial functions expanded. Therefore, the IMF set up the extended fund facility (EFF) in 1974 to assist members that experienced serious payment imbalances relating to structural maladjustments in production, trade, and prices and that intended to implement corrective policies for two to three years. Furthermore, using borrowed resources, the IMF created two oil facilities (1974 and 1975) to help members meet the increased cost of oil imports and products, on the one side, and provided supplementary financing facilities (SFF) to supplement the ordinary resources, on the other. After the SFF had been fully committed by 1982 similar provisions continued under the enlarged access policy.

Even though the price of oil rose dramatically, the international system survived the first shock quite successfully. The disequilibriums were financed effectively largely through the recycling of petrodollars and through the fund's two oil facilities. Thus, when the second oil crisis hit the world in 1979, it was widely expected that it would have the same outcome as that of 1973. Yet it was soon all but obvious to observers that history was not going to repeat itself. First, commercial banks had already lent heavily to developing countries. Second, the fund did not create any new low-condition oil facilities after 1979. Third, globally increasing interest rates, as a result of deflationary monetary and fiscal policies in the major industrial countries to counter inflation, made it difficult for developing countries to service their debts and to take out new loans. Finally, due to the widespread business depression in 1981 and 1982 developing countries suffered a sharp fall in their export prices in relation not only to oil prices, but to the prices of imported goods (i.e., a worsening of their "terms of trade"). The credit crunch in the United States led to an unmerciful recession, reflected by a downturn in commodity prices, which caught debtors in the classic "scissors effect" of higher debt service and decreased export income.[1]

Developing countries initially financed their current account deficits by borrowing from transnational banks. But this simply increased their foreign debts and eventually triggered the international debt crisis.[2] For instance, between 1972 and 1982 outstanding debt of Latin American countries to financial intermediaries rose from about $20 billion to about $214 billion. Thus, after 1982 the scale of the debt crisis reached such a dangerous level that major changes in the international monetary system became inevitable. As Barston puts it, "Not only were there no established institutional arrangements to cope with the scale of debt restructuring or renegotiations, no single institution or state grouping was capable of providing unaided the necessary financial resources to meet the needs of deficit countries" (Barston, 1988: 145). This deficiency of international problem management would, however, disappear with the institutionalization of the so-called Paris Club and London Club, respectively.[3]

---

1. The view here is that a series of exogenous events eventually triggered the international debt crisis. Dornbusch, however, argues that external adverse factors were not the only influence. Instead, "domestic policies were an important, often the main, influence in bringing about a large accumulation of debt" (Dornbusch, 1989: 342).

2. There is agreement that the international debt crisis goes back to August 1982, when Mexico informed the international financial community that it could no longer service its debts. However, Poland (1981) and Argentina (1982) had already declared a moratorium earlier. But it was the enormous size of Mexico's external debt ($63 billion by 1982) that surprised international financial markets. The global debt crisis is also regarded as largely a Latin American affair, because it was the huge size of their debt that threatened the stability of the international financial system.

3. While debt negotiations between sovereign borrowers and public lenders are dealt with in the Paris Club, restructurings between sovereign debtors and private creditors are conducted within the framework of the London Club. The London Club is officially the Commercial Bank Advisory Committees, but has been renamed by the media to distinguish it from the Paris Club.

DEBT CRISIS MANAGEMENT

The initial approach to the external debt-servicing crisis was through multiyear debt reschedulings (MYRAs) to cover amortizing payments on medium-term and long-term debt. These restructurings normally involved the safeguarding of spreads and fees similar to those of the initial debt, the restructuring of principal repayments over a long-term perspective, and the rolling over of maturities. Initially, it was also agreed to exclude interest payments on outstanding debts from rescheduling so as not to impair future access to international capital markets. The restructuring measures were usually tied to adjustment programs advocated by the IMF as well as concerted bank lending packages that increased bank exposure to a debtor country equiproportionally. It was believed that "new money" would, on the one hand, raise a debtor's future debt-servicing capacity through all kinds of investment and, on the other, decrease the so-called free rider problem through a pari passu or sharing clause in syndicated loan agreements.[1] By 1985, fifty-two (successful) bank reschedulings had been conducted through advisory or steering committees of the London Club.

Even though this approach proved important for the continued need of financial resources and for the maintenance of cohesion among financial intermediaries, it was not the only private response to the international debt problem. In May 1987, Citibank introduced a new era by reserving $3 billion out of its total exposure of about $13 billion to debtor countries—a move that eventually triggered rounds of reserve-taking steps by all major transnational banks. In fact, Citibank's unilateral response to the debt problem meant a serious blow to the "new money" approach, better known as the Baker Plan, arguing that new commitments of money from banks would lead debtors back on the road to prosperity. What came in April 1989 in place of the Baker Plan was the so-called Brady Plan which implied that debt reduction—as opposed to rescheduling—would be necessary to overcome the debt crisis. As a result, by 1993 the majority of the transnational banks had reserved or sold almost all of their debts, although the Europe-based financial intermediaries fared somewhat better than their Anglo-Saxon peers.

The rationale behind the Brady Plan was that the 1982 crisis was not a liquidity but an insolvency crisis, suggesting that financial intermediaries sell and write off their exposure at a loss rather than participate in further rounds of lending. The introduction of the secondary market for sovereign debt, however, happened rather discreetly and behind closed doors. Nobody was really interested in letting emerge an official price for these sovereign debts. On the one hand, the private actors feared increased pressure from debtor countries, which might push for further con-

---

1. These clauses oblige debtors to distribute their debt-service payments to creditors according to the latter's share in the initial syndicated loan.

cessions—a valid concern given the significant discounts that were unofficially granted—and on the other, creditors wanted to prevent regulators from asking them to value their credit portfolios at "unofficial" prices that would have been too much to take. A rather common instrument used in the secondary market were the so-called debt–equity swaps, which allowed a transnational company to buy sovereign debt in the secondary market and then change it into the currency with the central bank in order to invest directly in a domestic project.

Clearly, it was the rounds of reserve taking that made it possible for the financial intermediaries to sign the Brady Plan, thus contributing to the solution of the international debt crisis. The credits were transformed in easily tradable bonds with maturities of usually thirty years. The creditors, in turn, would agree on discounts on the face value or make concessions on future interest payments. The Brady Plan thus opened the door for a new class of investors to engage in emerging markets. In contrast to the market for credits, which was extremely illiquid due to a plethora of complications such as fees and treaties, the Brady bond markets were much easier to enter.

THE MAKING OF A TRANSNATIONAL REGIME:
THE LONDON CLUB

It is never in the interest of financial intermediaries that a debtor declares its inability to meet its financial obligations[1]—neither in an illiquidity crisis (temporary insolvency; liabilities are covered by assets) nor in an insolvency crisis (losses are inevitable; liabilities are not fully covered by assets). The goal of all transnational banks is therefore to prevent a voluntary default, an involuntary default, or a financial crisis. Yet because of the different size of the outstanding credits and different risk exposures—not every creditor is equally interested in the rescue of a debtor—the banking community is anything but a homogenous group. Accordingly, the so-called free rider problem occurs, which was especially manifest in the Mexican case.[2] In 1982, more than 530 banks agreed on new funds, whereas in 1987 only 400 financial actors wanted to participate in the Mexican rescue, of which 65 refused to provide new funds.

The emergence of the free rider problem lies in the fact that the provision of new funds as well as write-offs are public goods. Nonproduced, everlasting, or self-renewing goods do not have to be reproduced and hence do not create a public goods

---

1. Eaton and Gersovitz have always urged transnational creditors to work together to minimize the incentive of a potential debtor to declare default (Eaton and Gersovitz, 1981: 36).

2. For a detailed account of the restructuring packages in the Mexican and Brazilian cases, see Mendelsohn (1983); and Kraft (1984).

dilemma. Yet all the other goods inevitably lead to a "public goods dilemma" or the "problem of collective action."[1] This can be conferred from "nonexcludability," one of the dilemma's two properties (its other property is the joint supply by the public), which means that an actor may enjoy the benefits of public goods without having to contribute to their provisions. Therefore, once public goods are freely accessible and the shift from exclusion to inclusion is set free, the dilemma naturally emerges.

Clearly, this holds true in the case of new lending and debt relief à la Brady (Sachs, 1984; Swoboda, 1985). If there is an illiquidity crisis, both the provision of funds and debt reduction become public goods. For example, when new money is paid every creditor will be better off, even those that have not provided new money.[2] Similarly, if one party forgives some debt, the value of the remaining debt rises because the debtor is now in a much better situation to deliver on its obligation. The resulting benefit would, however, serve only those actors that preferred not to agree on debt relief. The same holds true in the case of buybacks of debt. Suppose that a debtor country offers to buy back some of its outstanding debt in the secondary market. If the creditor agrees on the deal, the value of the remaining debt on the market will inevitably increase, which again accrues considerable benefits to those parties that did not participate in the initial deal.

How can this problem be properly approached? Basically, there are two ways: by force or by making the decision of a potential free rider, a determinant of the final result. In the first case, it is common practice to speak of "involuntary" or "concerted" lending or debt relief, meaning that creditor banks are forced into either providing new money or writing off debt. This has been done by large financial intermediaries, which have performed a policing role, or the IMF, which has been acting as an "organizing agent" for transnational banks (Swoboda, 1985: 158). The second way, on the other hand, usually involves the introduction of unanimous voting in the rescheduling process. Even though a creditor thus has a right of veto, unanimity ensures that the decision of a potential free rider determines the outcome of the overall result. Initially, the provision of new credits, for instance, was based on unanimous decisions; only later did the creditor banks agree on a new decision-making procedure with a quorum ("critical mass") of 90 percent. But, as Swoboda correctly remarks, these two steps involve more emergency responses than long-term measures. A more optimal response would involve a "precommitment by club members to actions" (ibid.: 159). The establishment of the Institute of International

---

1. Barry and Hardin go to great lengths to distinguish between the dilemma of public goods and the problem of collective action (Barry and Hardin, 1982: 32). But there is no obvious reason for employing two definitions when one would do perfectly.

2. This logic also applies to the case of insolvency, because losses on new credits are practically certain.

Finance, for instance, can be seen as a step toward such a solution.[1] However, the much more effective and far-reaching response to the public goods dilemma has been—and still is—the formation of advisory or steering committees.[2]

By creating these committees, transnational banks, drawing from their prior ties and institutional arrangements, have come up with a regime that helps them formulate common positions and succeed in getting smaller and less exposed banks in line. Of course, their establishment seems plausible, but they are quite difficult to create. Rescheduling debt is a highly complicated task that involves a variety of distinct actors. There is no a priori harmony of interest, but instead, smaller banks maintain different ties and links to one another or have other interests and roles than do transnational banks. Thus, even if a final decision is eventually reached they are often reluctant to provide their proper share; sometimes they explicitly threaten to defect. Despite these problems creditor banks have demonstrated great capacity to manage their differences in reaching joint action. Hence, as Lipson correctly underscores,

The larger point to be emphasized . . . is not the conflicting preferences about the form of new credits, but the capacity of large private banks to coordinate effectively in cases of troubled debt despite their differences, and despite their vigorous competition as Euromarket lenders. (Lipson, 1985: 214)

The capacity of transnational actors—against popular opinion—to help each other overcome an international financial crisis is so cardinal that their far-reaching cooperation needs to be explained in greater detail.

Lipson has shown that the process of creating an advisory committee usually involves two steps (ibid.: 204–14). First, transnational banks convene to bargain over the general terms of rescheduling, and then urge smaller creditors to assent. Although smaller banking institutes might be unwilling to approve such rescheduling terms over which they have had no influence, large creditors are nonetheless in the driver's seat. In daily life they have provided smaller banks with such a wide range of financial services and products that their long-term financial relationships virtually guarantee cooperation on the part of the smaller creditors. Moreover, they break the rescheduling game into a series of bilateral games, thus confronting

---

1. Mendelsohn (1983) provides a short, but sufficient description of the Institute of International Finance (the Ditchley group).

2. In the Mexican case, the first meeting of the advisory committee was held on 20 August 1982 in the Citibank building in New York City. On hand were thirteen financial intermediaries: Bank of America, Bank of Montreal, Bank of Tokyo, Bankers Trust, Banomex of Mexico, Chase Manhattan, Chemical Bank, Deutsche Bank, Lloyds, ManTrust, Morgan Guaranty, Société Générale, and Swiss Bank Corporation. For a more detailed account, see Kraft (1984).

Table 3.1
Country Risk Rating (0 = worst; 100 = best)

Country	Euromoney		Institutional Investor	
	September 1996	September 1989	September 1996	September 1989
Argentina	57.3	28.0	38.9	19.0
Brazil	56.8	32.0	38.3	27.8
Chile	77.4	41.0	61.2	33.6
Colombia	62.4	37.0	46.7	36.9
Mexico	60.3	44.0	41.6	30.3

Note: Data based on *Euromoney, Institutional Investor.*

potential free riders with the key players. The rationale of this technique is, as Lipson claims, "that noncooperation is transparent; that defectors may be discriminated against in the future; and that the asymmetry of bank size permits effective, low-cost sanctions" (ibid.: 220).

How exactly does a transnational regime come into being? Usually, a debtor that is unable to meet its obligations contacts one or more of its larger creditors and asks for alterations in the terms of the initial loan. It might even try to elicit additional funds from its major creditors to meet its most exigent short-term commitments. The leading creditors then approach other large lenders and, if there is agreement on the need for rescheduling, form an advisory committee, including the biggest banks from all major financial centers. These transnational banks are "large enough to cover major national banking networks, but small enough to operate effectively" (ibid.: 217). For example, when Mexico's debt was rescheduled, the Bank of Tokyo was in charge of managing the Asian-based banks, whereas the Bank of Montreal was responsible for the Canadian banks.

Once the advisory committee is formed, its members devote their time to acquiring available financial data, which will serve as the surveyor's wooden rod on which to base the common strategy for the negotiation process and the size of future lendings or write-offs. The next order of business is to proceed with the ratification of the rescheduling agreement (ibid.: 214–20). First, together with the debtor, the committee devises a draft agreement that it also might table to other creditors if need be. The usual method in such a case would be regional meetings at which the debtor's key officials participate as well. Before the final document is formulated, the initial draft will be cleared by the smaller banks for any kind of concerns they may voice. After the agreement has been finalized, the debtor country eventually invites all creditors of the generally agreed upon terms, which have been supported by the advisers and others (e.g., IMF), and calls on them to ratify the document. It then asks the committee members, if need be, for payment of their pro rata share within a certain period.

By way of summary, it can be said that the formation of the advisory committees has enabled the financial intermediaries to master state insolvencies. This regime has provided the actors with a forum to cooperate with each other and thereby overcome the public goods dilemma. Even though some economists claim that it was the enormous pressure of the United States that essentially prevented a blow to the international monetary system posed by the international debt crisis (Sachs, 1986), it would be mistaken to deny the vital role played by the transnational banks in thwarting a global financial crisis.[1] It is doubtful that the crisis would have been overcome so "easily" without the steering committees; they have provided new funds and forced debt write-offs on members as a consequence of the Brady Plan by bringing into line free riders.[2]

THE ROAD TO SUCCESS LEADS TO THE LONDON CLUB

The beneficial effects of the London Club can be shown by referring to macroeconomic key figures. For instance, in terms of inflation, the Latin American

---

1. A less known but not least important transnational regime in connection with the management of emerging market debt is the multilateral netting facility, established by eleven members of the Emerging Markets Traders Association (EMTA) for 136 Russian credits with a face value of $341 million. The reason for setting up this arrangement was to reduce settlement delays of sovereign debt. Today EMTA, which is an association of about seventy transnational financial operators based in New York, is working for a more effective netting scheme. Against the background of the increasing prominence of emerging market debt instruments in the global financial world, the formation of a more efficient netting arrangement is quite reasonable. For instance, trade volume in bonds of emerging markets has meanwhile more than doubled to about $2 billion, whereas the volume of Brady bonds was almost four times as large as in 1993.

2. In this context it is worthwhile to take notice of the so-called Baker Initiative Committee (BIC). It is an ad hoc group of financial intermediaries that convenes from time to time with central banks and officials from multilateral organizations to discuss sovereign debt. The BIC was formed in the mid-1980s at the height of the international debt crisis. Essentially, officials of the European Bank of Reconstruction and Development (EBRD), International Development Bank (IDB), IMF, and the World Bank meet with representatives of financial intermediaries and inform them about their work and suggest what private lenders can do to resolve problems of indebted and emerging economies.

countries have been rather successful as price increases have been significantly reduced and brought back under control (Credit Suisse Research, 1996). In fact, Argentina and Brazil curbed inflation in 1995 to a remarkably low level of 1.6 percent (2,313 percent in 1990) and 23.2 percent (1,638 percent in 1990), respectively, and reduced the more important external debt burden. According to Credit Suisse, the total debt-service ratio (interest payment plus principle amortization over exports of goods and services) for Latin America has declined from an approximately 37 percent in the early 1980s to approximately 30 percent in 1995. This improvement also found confirmation in a significant recovery of the secondary market. For instance, Argentinean debt was traded at 22 percent of face value in September 1988, at 69 percent in December 1993, and at 60 percent in December 1995, while Mexican bonds were priced at 47 in September 1988, at 84 in 1993, and at 65 in December 1995. Finally, the debt recovery also led to an improvement in the country risk assessments by private rating agencies, such as Moody's and Standard and Poor's, and financial intermediaries[1] (Table 3.1).

The improvements were so strong that not even the 1994–1995 Mexican crisis, which led to a devaluation of the Mexican peso, could derail this process. In fact, as IBCA, one of the world's top three credit-rating agencies, wrote in its comment on the Mexican crisis:

there [were] fundamental differences between Mexico's present position and its position in 1982. Mexico's gross external debt [was] worth some 230 percent of exports of goods, services and income compared with 332 percent in 1982 and a peak ratio of 374 percent in 1986. As a percentage of GDP, gross external debt has fallen from 60 percent in 1982 to 41 percent in 1994. Moreover, the policy fundamentals [were] better. Inflation [was] 6.9 percent, when it averaged 59 percent in 1982 and reached 99 percent at the end of that year. The government's own finances [were] also much improved: the public sector borrowing requirement in 1981 was 14 percent of GDP and reached 16.9 percent of GDP in 1982. . . . Exports have been rising despite worries about an overvalued exchange rate. Direct investment has established a substantial export-oriented manufacturing base aimed at the U.S. and Canadian markets, to which Mexico now has free access under the North American Free Trade Agreement (NAFTA). . . . These gains have not been thrown away by the present crisis. (*IBCA*, 30 December 1994)

True, other Latin American countries initially came under intense pressure (Credit Suisse First Boston, 1995: 22–23). But the fear that the Mexican crisis could spill over to other economies in the region was unwarranted. Many specific causes of its currency crisis were not shared by the other countries. The peso was regarded as considerably overvalued by 20 to 30 percent, which led to an unsustainably huge deficit on the current account of the balance of payments. These deficits were

---

1. *Institutional Investor* has developed country-by-country credit ratings based on information provided by leading transnational bankers, who are asked to grade the countries listed on a scale of zero (worst) to 100 (best).

mainly financed by attracting short-term foreign capital, including investments in *cetes*, *tesobonos*, and Mexican equity. Furthermore, Mexican banks issued dollar-denominated certificates of deposits (CDs) and onlent the resources at higher interest rates to onshore borrowers. The short-term debt obligations of Mexico thus amounted to $44 billion, which corresponded to virtually 2.5 times the foreign exchange reserves held by the Mexican central bank. Another reason why Mexico's troubles did not result in a regional debt crisis is that the net amount of funds that flowed into Latin America between 1978 and 1981 was approximately 57 percent larger in real terms than between 1990 and 1993. Moreover, the recipients of the recent inflow were largely actors from the private sector rather than from the financial and public sectors as during the first boom years. Finally, unlike in the late 1970s and early 1980s, it was not bank loans but direct and portfolio investment that boosted development.

DEBT ACCORD UNDER THE LONDON CLUB: EXAMPLES

The success of the London Club did not go unnoticed. Recently, the geographic scope of the club was extended to eastern Europe and northern Africa. Arguably the most heavily discussed deal recently struck under the aegis of the London Club were the two debt accords with Poland in March and September 1994. The first deal restructured old bank loans into long-term debt, which Poland felt able to service, whereas the second deal halved Poland's defaulted $13.8 billion transnational debt. Factually, the September deal envisaged two options: either the loans were immediately bought back by Poland or they were transformed into thirty-year interest-bearing Brady bonds. Banks that chose the first option were promptly paid on 27 October 1994, though with a significant discount of 59 to 62 cents per U.S. dollar for medium- and long-term debt and revolving trade debt, respectively. Given the huge discount, more than two-thirds of the banks opted for the Brady bond version. These bonds, however, yield different returns, depending on the specific bond categories. The so-called par bonds and the past due interest bonds yield a return of 12.56 percent, while the discount bonds pay 13.44 percent. The deal was that the discount bonds—unlike in the first option—would be paid 55 cents per U.S. dollar rather than only 41 cents. In addition, these Brady bonds hold the promise of repaying one dollar for the initially paid 55 cents in 30 years. This works because the Polish government is obliged to buy 30-year U.S. treasury bills (i.e., zero bonds) through a trust company that currently cost 14 percent. These discount bonds are then redeemed with the 100 percent payback. Thanks to this security, bond holders have the guarantee that the Poland bonds will actually be paid back, although interest payments are not covered by this deal. This goes to show that restructuring deals not only provide stability by bringing all lenders together to write off some part of their credits, but also make it possible for an emerging economy to rejoin the global financial community. Transnational lenders shied away from Poland as it could not repay bank loans it already owed. However, with the financing avenues open, funding of much needed improvements of nationwide infrastructure programs was made both easier and cheaper.

An equally publicized London Club arrangement was the one with Bulgaria on 28 July 1994.[1] After more than two years of intense negotiations, Bulgaria signed a market-based debt and debt-service reduction deal with more than three hundred commercial banks. The agreement resulted in the $8.3 billion restructuring of bank debt and a thirty-year period repayment schedule. The exchange of old debt for new bonds considerably improved Bulgaria's situation: its debt overhang has been reduced, its maturity profile ameliorated, and its attractiveness to foreign investors increased. Under the restructuring deal, Bulgaria's debt and debt-service were reduced by about 46 percent in present value terms, and the ratio of scheduled debt-service to export income was considerably lowered to a projected peak of about 20 to 24 percent over the medium term. The IMF reckons that the buyback equivalent price of the deal (i.e., the cost per unit of debt and debt-service reduction) at 19 percent was significantly under the prevailing secondary market price for Bulgarian debt. Compared to other debt-restructuring deals, Bulgaria's debt and debt-service reduction was higher than the weighted average of all previous deals (39 %), between that of Mexico (45 %) and Poland (49 %). The buyback equivalent price, on the other hand, was extremely low compared to other deals and the weighted average (34 cents).

The London Club has also struck a deal with Algeria. On 12 May 1995, it agreed with the Algerian central bank to reschedule $3.3 billion of commercial bank debt. It has been arranged that repayment of loans would begin in 1998. The deal, which carries an interest of 81 basis points over Libor, has been split into four separate deals for different types of debt. The previously reprofiled facilities with original maturities between one and two years as well as the reprofiled leasing transactions will be repaid in fifteen equal semiannual installments between September 1998 and September 2005. For all the other debt, the London Club decided that the repayment would be in twenty equal semiannual installments from September 2000 to March 2010. The closing agent was Union de Banques Arabes & Françaises, whereby the other steering committee members were Société Générale, Sakura Bank, Arab Banking Corporation, Japan Leasing Corporation, Chase Manhattan Bank, and Long Term Credit Bank of Japan.

On 21 November 1996 the Ivory Coast became the latest debtor country to negotiate a Brady-style restructuring. This is the result of an agreement with the London Club that renegotiated $7.2 billion of Ivorian obligations—amounting to

---

1. See *International Monetary Fund Survey* (1995: 230–32).

approximately 40 percent of the country's outstanding external debt of 17 billion. Some $4.6 billion of the debt stemmed from interest arrears that had accumulated since April 1987, when the Ivory Coast honored its obligations last. The debt forgiveness implied by this London Club agreement amounted to about 80 percent of principal and past due interest. The terms of the club rescheduling involved the following steps. First, the Ivory Coast would buy back approximately 30 percent of principal at 24 cents a dollar. Second, two instruments were issued at the discretion of the creditors: a 30-year discount bond with 50 percent upfront principal reduction and low fixed-rate coupons of 2.5 percent to 4 percent for the first 10 years, rising to 13/16ths over Libor for the last 20 years; and a 20-year amortizing front-loaded interest-reduction par bond (FLIRB) with step-up, fixed coupons of 2 percent to 5 percent for the first 14 years, rising to 13/16ths over Libor for the remaining 6 years. There would also be a 20-year amortizing past due interest bond with coupons of 2 percent for the first 10 years, 3 percent for the next five years, and 13/16ths over Libor for the remaining 5 years. This bond would replace the 70 percent of interest arrears that had not been canceled by the buyback and recalculated at Libor minus 2 percent.

The Senegalese government also benefited from a London Club agreement. The deal that became effective on 23 December 1996 covered the country's commercial debt of $118 million, including $75 million of principal. It provided for a cash buy-back of the principal at 16 percent with foregiveness of the related interest. The deal also offered an alternative in form of an exchange for non-interest bearing long-term payment instruments issued at par which would be secured by zero-coupon U.S. Treasury bonds with a maturity of 28 years. It is envisaged that these instruments could be used as a means of payment in various debt conversion programs. Given the historical links with France, the steering committee, which consisted of Citibank, Crédit Lyonnais, and Société Générale, was headed by Banque Nationale de Paris. The agreement was well received by the international financial community as it restored the confidence in Senegal.

4

Netting Schemes

When you are faced with speculation, the only thing to do is to make them pay the price for their speculation. During the [French] Revolution, such people were known as agioteurs and they were beheaded.

—M. Michel Sapin

The exchange rates of the major economies have been free to float since the breakdown of the Bretton Woods system of fixed exchange rates in 1973. What has been happening ever since are large swings in currencies. Exchange rates have tended to overshoot or undershoot significantly over time. Why have these tremendous fluctuations come about, and what have been their driving forces? This is a tricky question as the rationale behind the transition from a fixed to a floating exchange rate system has been the ability of governments to recapture the use of monetary policy for domestic economic management. But more important, it was assumed that exchange rates would move "automatically" to reflect changes in relative prices, on the one hand, and that real exchange rates[1] would be consequently more stable and trade imbalances smaller. This in turn would strengthen the global economic and political system. Yet the new foreign exchange regime proved a disappointment for central bankers. Foreign currencies tended to appreciate in economies with trade deficits and high inflation and to fluctuate by more than was needed to balance relative price movements. Rather than blaming the currency

---

1. Real exchange rates are defined as the nominal exchange rates adjusted for inflation differences.

volatility on financial speculation[1] and the inefficient behavior of the foreign exchange (forex) markets, economics provided an elegant explanation.

Explaining exchange rate volatility, Dornbusch (1976) merged the monetary and asset market approaches into a sophisticated understanding of the causes of exchange rate movements. Accordingly, Dornbusch holds that in the short term, exchange rates are determined by the assets markets, while in the long term, rates are governed by the purchasing power parity (PPP). In other words, exchange rate changes are moving in line with relative inflation rates. If America's inflation rate is, say, 3 percent, and that of the United Kingdom 4 percent, the dollar must increase by one percent a year against the pound. Even though PPP is economically logical, it has failed to forecast exchange rates accurately. The reason is that capital flows have not been taken into account. A remedy was found in the asset market approach, which argues that capital flows are more influential than trade flows in determining exchange rates. If capital is free to flow where it is "treated" best, exchange rates will move until the moment when the total expected returns[2] from each currency are equal. Thus, exchange rates will move when interest rate differentials change or when investors' expectations about future forex rates change.

Even though Dornbusch has provided proof that forex markets are efficient and rational, politicians, regulators, and some academics still believe that currency rates are much too important to be left to the markets. They believe that the free-floating system enables traders either to upset stable currency alignments or put the international financial system at risk through speculation in forex markets. Knowing that a second Bretton Woods system is not realistic, the "anti-floaters" have therefore come up with proposals aimed at taming the forex markets. In the aftermath of the European Monetary System (EMS) breakdown, Eichengreen and Wyplosz (1993), for instance, proposed a sort of "implicit tax" on forex transactions to slow down foreign exchange markets and thus enable distressed governments to realign their attacked currencies.[3] Both scholars drew heavily from earlier proposals, such as the interest equalization tax (Cooper, 1965) and the Tobin tax (Tobin, 1978). Interestingly enough, even Dornbusch (1986) recommended "speed limits" for world financial markets to make them more stable. Last but not least, Schau-

---

1. In the economic sense, speculation is only dangerous when speculators are following market movements rather than acting on sound fundamentals. Otherwise, speculative activities are important in a market economy as they support the market mechanism by reducing risks. Speculators take positions commensurate with their expectations and thus help stabilize price movements.

2. Total expected returns are here defined as interest plus the expected depreciation or appreciation.

3. Together with Tobin, Eichengreen and Wyplosz modified their original arguments by elaborating in more detail the "implicit tax" on credits granted to foreigners (1995).

mayer, former governor of the Austrian National Bank, came out in favor of putting more prudential control on the activities of the foreign exchange markets. She argued that the market participants should be required to report their net forex positions on a daily rather than monthly basis to central banks in order to check their positions. In this respect, the Basle Committee on Banking Supervision already discussed a capital charge of 8 percent of net open position to be imposed for engaging in forex risks.[1] It is assumed that this measurement would significantly reduce daily turnover of the forex markets. Even though the above ideas emphasize different aspects, they have one thing in common: they all address the presumed disturbances that wreck the carefully laid plans to establish firm control over international financial markets. But are these criticisms really justified? Does the free-floating system put the international monetary system at risk? Does it beguile forex traders into attacking the international reserves of weak currency countries or into speculation as it promises huge swings and thus huge profits?

RISKS IN FOREX MARKETS

Insofar as the presumed loss of official control over forex rates is concerned, it is not so much the free markets or the supposedly mean forex dealers that cause currency overshootings or realignments within currency systems, as much as the policies of the governments themselves (see Appendix 3). In fact, the free-floating system merely rewards sound monetary and fiscal policies and forces changes on inflationary ones. Therefore, although speculators make easy scapegoats, the official policies have to be blamed when financial markets turn "chaotic." Forex markets know all too well that "speculative" attacks on supposedly weak currencies could easily backfire, as the Austrian case in August 1993 nicely revealed when dealers had to buy back their schillings very dearly to cover their short positions.

Not every policymaker or regulator, however, blames the forex markets for the derailment of their ill-chosen policies. There is also the officialdom that is not unduly ignorant about forex markets and their implicit risks and realizes that it is not so much the attacks on currencies—particularly in the light of the provisions of hedging products—but the huge volumes that threaten the international system.[2] For instance, daily forex volume transacted in London alone had reached $464 billion in 1995, whereas New York recorded an average of $244 billion. Tokyo, the third biggest financial center, has reached the remarkable level of $161 billion (BIS, 1996). Against this background, it comes as no surprise that forex participants could easily experience substantial losses if one of their counterparts were to

---

1. For a more detailed discussion, see Shirreff (1993: 60–69); and Eichengreen and Wyplosz (1993: 51–124).

2. See especially Gilbert (1992).

declare its inability to settle its side of the transaction.[1] It is, therefore, quite understandable that regulators around the world shudder at the thought of such "systemic risks."

Whether a unilateral declaration of a party's inability to pay necessarily leads to a loss depends on the financial condition of the defaulting counterparty. For instance, a solvent financial intermediary may default because of operating problems, making it impossible for it to execute its payments. It may lack the proper currency on the value date, or it may simply forget to execute instructions. Such liquidity risks[2] normally do not put the international system at great risk due to their temporary nature. It often happens that the central bank steps in with short-term loans and thus helps solve the liquidity problem. Bankruptcy and ensuing liquidation of a financial intermediary,[3] on the other hand, pose a serious threat to the international financial market by causing systemic disruptions. One incident that might cause a system-wide breakdown is the default of a participant in the foreign currency markets where credit and liquidity risks are constantly imminent at any given time. This can be shown nicely by the theoretical concept of the prisoner's dilemma.

The reason for the public goods or prisoner's dilemma to emerge in forex trading lies in the specific nature of such transactions. First, they are so-called spot-and-forward contracts, involving nonsimultaneous or noninstantaneous contributions. Second, they are not self-enforcing, and third, they do not allow for any kind of reliance. This fact seemingly puts the international monetary system at some risk. This predicament is, however, considerably circumvented by financial intermediaries. On the one side, continuing interactions with more or less the same players mean that self-restraint today will pay inevitable returns tomorrow; on the other, financial intermediaries have established transnational regimes (the so-called net-

---

1. This risk is also referred to as the Herstatt risk. It arises because of the nature of settlement of forex transactions. A settlement involves a cash transfer from one party's account to another party's account in the country of the respective currency. Because those parties are located in different time zones, there may be a delay of payments. For instance, if a party buys D-marks against U.S. dollars, it receives the German currency before it transfers its dollars to its counterparty due to different office hours. As with regard to the defaulting Herstatt Bank, German regulators shut the bank after it already received D-marks, but before it delivered its dollars. Consequently, U.S. financial intermediaries found themselves in a liquidity squeeze that subsequently led to a liquidity crisis in the financial system. (See *Economist*, 7 May 1994)

2. Liquidity risk occurs when a counterparty will not settle an obligation on due day, but at an unknown date thereafter.

3. This risk is called credit risk and arises when a counterparty fails to settle an obligation for full value when due or thereafter.

Table 4.1
Comparison and Differences between Gross Settlement and Bilateral Netting

Parties	Gross Settlement	Bilateral Netting
Party A and B Deal 1: $1 = DM 1.80 Deal 2: $1 = DM 1.75	Party A to B: $100.00 Party B to A: DM 180.00 Party A to B: DM 87.50 Party B to A: $50.00	Party A to B: $50.00 Party B to A: DM 92.50
Party A and C Deal 3: $1 = DM 1.65 Deal 4: $1 = DM 1.75	Party A to C: $100.00 Party C to A: DM 165.00 Party A to C: DM 131.25 Party C to A: $75.00	Party A to C: $25.00 Party C to A: DM 33.75
Party B and C Deal 5: $1 = DM 1.72 Deal 6: $1 = DM 1.78	Party B to C: $150.00 Party C to B: DM 258.00 Party B to C: DM 178.00 Party C to B: $100.00	Party B to C: $50.00 Party C to B: DM 80.00

ting schemes) which—despite brisk competition and huge turnover—provide considerable risk provisions (i.e., minimize credit risks inherent in currency transactions by holding down their asset and liability balances), thus contributing to order and stability in the global financial market.[1] They do so by entering onto their balance sheets the difference between amounts payable and receivable of currency transactions rather than entering separately the total payable and the total receivable.

In fact, in order to absorb these tremendous capital flows, the private market has created systems to render cross-border payments as efficiently as possible.[2] As it turned out, huge capital flows made it impractical to hold accounts with all the other transnational operators. Consequently, money center operators took on the role of clearing and settlement agents for the smaller correspondent players. These money center actors would have access to national settlement procedures and hold accounts with their home central banks. Thus, they would supply liquidity to correspondent banks by providing collateralized or uncollateralized credit lines. In other

---

1. Similar schemes are also set up for the global securities markets. See, for instance, Group of Thirty (1990); and BIS (1992).

2. See especially Padoa-Schioppa and Saccomanni (1994: 235-68).

words, as clearing agents these money center banks would help "domesticize" cross-border payments. The enormous growth in cross-border transactions, however, made these money center banks opt for the more efficient netting schemes, thus becoming de facto multilateral clearing houses. The major reason for creating netting schemes for the purpose of the arrangement of interbank payments and financial contracts is the improvement of the efficiency of payment and settlement systems. It is to cut back on settlement costs as well as reduce credit risks and liquidity risks they face as they engage in financial transactions.

Why are these netting institutions believed to reduce systemic risk, that is, to increase the stability of the global monetary system? By reducing both the overall value of payments and the number between financial intermediaries, netting schemes increase the efficiency of national payment systems and reduce settlement costs common to the huge and ever-growing size of forex transactions. At the same time, they reduce the size of credit and liquidity exposures assumed by market participants and thus contribute to the containment of systemic risk.

EFFECTS OF NETTING ARRANGEMENTS

If netting schemes are to reduce the volume of payments and settlement risks, there must be at least two parties engaged in two deals in the case of bilateral netting and three parties engaged in six deals plus a central clearing house through which the payments are channeled in the case of multilateral netting. Suppose, then, that three forex dealers (Parties A, B, and C) engage in foreign exchange dealing in U.S. dollars and D-marks. Each party does forex deals with the other, whereby each pair of parties is engaged in two transactions. In the first deal, a party transfers dollars in exchange for D-marks, while paying D-marks for dollars in the second deal. The first deal is negotiated at 1$ = DM 1.80, the second at 1$ = DM 1.75. The exchange rate at value date is 1$ = DM 1.70, thus creating profits and losses.[1] In addition to the different rates, the transactions also diverge in size, which therefore leads to imbalances in the transfer payments of currencies between the parties. (The various deals and their respective forex rates are listed in Table 4.1).

The above circumscribed scenario provides an explanation of the effects involved in netting schemes. Under the traditional gross settlement the two forex dealers (Parties A and B) have to execute payment instructions for each single leg of the deal to settle their obligations. In the first case, Party A pays $100.00 to Party B, which pays DM 180.00 in turn. Since the forex rate at value date is 1$ = DM 1.70, Party A makes a profit of DM 10.00. In the second transaction Party A pays

---

1. Since the deals are negotiated in the spot market, they are negotiated two days before value date.

Figure 4.1
Multilateral Netting Arrangement

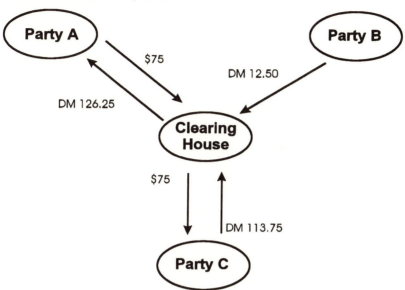

DM 87.50 to Party B, which transfers $50.00 in turn. Again, this deal yields a profit of DM 2.50, though for Party B. Under the more efficient bilateral netting scheme the number of payment instructions can, however, be reduced to only 2 with a total value of only DM 177.50. Party A pays $50.00, while receiving DM 92.50. If Party C joins the market, the loss exposure and transaction costs may be reduced even further by engaging in multilateral netting (Figure 4.1). Rather than involving 12 payments and a total value of DM 1,807.25, multilateral netting can reduce these instructions to 5 with a total value of DM 507.50.

The positive effects of multilateral netting arrangements with their clearing houses compared to the more simple over-the-counter (OTC) market in terms of counterparty risks and efficiency can also be exploited in the derivatives market for foreign currency products. Imagine a derivatives market with 100 participants engaging in 5 deals per day over the course of one year (240 business days) at a cost of $5 per transaction. In the OTC market there would be almost 6 million transactions, while in the case of a clearing house the number is only 24,000. The same is true for transaction costs. In the case of gross settlement the financial intermediaries have to pay almost $30 million, whereas in the case of multilateral netting the financial services industry pays only $120,000 (see Table 4.2). Obviously, the effects of netting arrangements depend on their institutional setups (see Figure 4.2).

Table 4.2
Gross (OTC) Netting versus Multilateral Netting

| Players | Transactions per year | | |
	Gross	Bilateral	Multilateral
10	54,000	10,800	2,400
50	1,470,000	294,000	12,000
100	5,940,000	1,188,000	24,000

| Players | Transaction costs per year ($) | | |
	Gross	Bilateral	Multilateral
10	270,000	54,000	12,000
50	7,350,000	1,470,000	60,000
100	29,700,000	5,940,000	120,000

Transactions: 5 per day
Costs: $5 per transaction
Trading days: 240 per year

TRANSNATIONAL REGIMES: NETTING SCHEMES

The institutional forms of netting arrangements differ with respect to their legal
character, to the net amounts due, to the existence of a central counterparty, and to
their bilateral or multilateral nature: (1) bilateral accounting/position netting; (2)
bilateral netting by novation; (3) multilateral position netting; and (4) multilateral
netting by novation and substitution (BIS, 1989; Zobl and Werlen, 1994). Bilateral
position netting is an arrangement under which two parties informally agree to
make only one net payment bilaterally between themselves for each currency and
value date for which amounts are due. This form of netting reduces the liquidity
risk because the netting calculation makes it possible to settle payments due from
a counterparty to offset payments due to this counterparty. As regards credit risks,
bilateral netting does not, however, cater for net amounts in the event of a
counterparty defaulting. It is assumed that a party experiencing financial squeezes
remains responsible for its gross obligation; accordingly, the gross amount under-

Figure 4.2
Systemic Efficiency and Systemic Stability

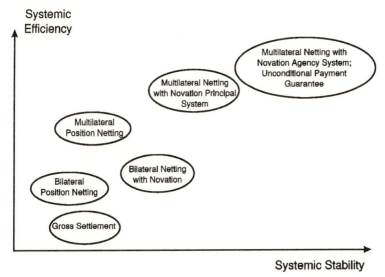

Source: Burkhard Varnholt, *Systemrisiken auf Finanzmärkten unter besonderer Berücksichtigung der Märkte für Derivative*, Bern: Haupt, 1995. Used by permission of Paul Haupt Publishers.

lying netted amounts is not extinguished. Thus, it follows that the parties remain ultimately responsible for all risks they assume.

Services providing for bilateral netting by novation[1] effect a reduction of the credit risk by discharging each individual forex contract as if it were netted ("obligation netting"). That is, amounts due under a discharged deal are added to the running balances due between the parties in each currency at each value date in the future. Netting by novation thus aims at reducing liquidity risks, on both the counterparty and its correspondent banks, and counterparty credit risks through the shift from gross to net basis in respect of any forward date. According to official figures, it is indeed feasible to achieve a reduction of more than 50 percent in terms of both the value and the number of payments (BIS, 1990: 11). A similar scheme is the so-called master agreement, principally applied to forex trading and interest swap deals. Such arrangements differ from netting by novation insofar as they incorporate several agreements between two parties into a single legal agreement, thus leading to a similar single net credit exposure as regards forward commitments. In contrast to novation, the individual deals are not incorporated into running

---

1. Two existing contracts between two parties for delivery of a certain currency on the same value date are replaced by only one net contract for that specific date, such that the first original two contracts are satisfied and discharged.

accounts, but rather keep their specific terms, rates, and maturities and thereby may be terminated individually.

In addition to bilateral netting arrangements, there is also the provision of netting on a multilateral basis. It is achieved by calculating the net position of all deals negotiated by each of the participants with each of the others, resulting in a single multilateral "net-net" position. The netting is then conducted by a central entity (i.e., clearing house) that is legally empowered to substitute for the original party to each deal. Thus, the net-net position will essentially be a bilateral net position between each party and the clearing house. The key point of multilateral netting is that "net amounts due to or due from each participant vis-à-vis the clearing group as a whole, for value on a given day, are calculated and then settled by transfers of monetary balances from net debtors to net creditors" (BIS, 1989: 16). There are basically two institutional forms. Multilateral position netting, for instance, is characterized by a central clearing party that either holds balances for or provides necessary funds to the participants to facilitate settlements. It does reduce liquidity risks relative to bilateral netting, leaving credit risk the same as if no netting schemes were in place. That is, all gross obligations or payment instructions remain outstanding until final settlement. The reporting of multilateral positions is only to give all parties an idea of how much is due from or due to the clearing group as a whole.

Multilateral netting by novation and substitution, on the other hand, would normally be provided by a forex clearing house.[1] It would be substituted by the counterparty to a pair of dealers that have submitted their contract to it, and as a result the obligations would be discharged. In addition, the central party would be charged with the task of keeping track of the running novated net position for the relevant currencies and value dates vis-à-vis each party. Consequently, for each of the sets of contracts that have to be netted, net amounts due to the clearing house from each party or vice versa, respectively, add up to the same as the multilateral net position of each party vis-à-vis the netting group as a whole. In regard to the several risks involved in forex trading, this netting form shows considerable attributal advantages. Payment flows and liquidity needs on an aggregate basis are reduced, and—if they are legally binding—lead to a reduction of the credit and liquidity exposure levels incurred by the active market participants. The BIS reckons that in contrast to gross settlement, private payment netting schemes may reduce the value of settlement payments as well as the number of payments by approximately 80 percent (BIS, 1990: 13), thus contributing greatly to systemic stability.

---

1. A contract between two parties is amended, while a third party performs the role of an intermediary creditor/debtor between these two parties. The amended contract is then novated in order to satisfy and discharge the original contract.

This is, however, only the case if the multilateral netting scheme has "clearly defined procedures for the management of credit risks and liquidity risks which specify respective responsibilities of the netting provider and the participants" (ibid.: 35). In fact, one of the major concerns regulators have about multilateral netting schemes is whether the clearing house would have ample financial resources in the case of a member defaulting. Yet the lender of last resort function is taken care of by the parties that post collateral with the clearing house in an amount at least equal to their respective exposures as in the case of centralized risk management[1] or spread the losses among the participants as in the case of decentralized risk management (ibid.: 36–38).[2] Of course, the "prepays" for the risk of the participants' own default by posting collateral does not per se prevent the clearing house from experiencing a bigger loss than the defaulting party's posted collateral. In a centralized system, the excess loss would therefore need to be allocated to the remaining parties and charged against their posted collateral. In the decentralized system, the surviving parties would have a contingent liability (off-balance sheet) to cover the credit losses resulting from a counterparty's failure.

The most famous netting arrangement up until now is the Foreign Exchange Netting (FXNET). Initially it was set up by Chemical Bank, but now it is operated by a number of large financial intermediaries in the form of a partnership. FXNET came to fame basically because of its institutionalized and formalized system of bilateral netting by novation and a "close-out" provision.[3] FXNET provides modelized agreements and the necessary computer software for transmission of financial messages, confirmation matching, and accounting. The usual procedure entails two steps: the potential member buys the software under a special license agreement from FXNET and then concludes bilateral netting arrangements with other FXNET members. The system, which started in London, has been extended to New York to allow not only for local netting, but for cross-border netting as well. Furthermore, in order to provide for better rationalization effects, FXNET has been

---

1. In the centralized risk management system, which is a collateral-based scheme, the clearing house becomes the counterparty to all participants. Each counterparty then has an exposure to the clearing house and vice versa, but does not have any direct exposure to any of the other parties. The clearing house thus becomes responsible for the risk management. In order to be able to check on members, it places a ceiling on each participant's exposures equal to the collateral posted.

2. In the case of decentralized risk management the individual parties retain significant responsibilities for credit decision making. Bilateral credit limits is the major risk management mechanism for limiting credit exposure rather than the collateral-based risk management mechanism.

3. "Netting by close-out" is an arrangement to settle all forex contracts not yet due (liabilities to and claims on a party) by one single payment, immediately, upon the event previously defined.

Table 4.3
Features of Netting Schemes

	FXNET	ISDA Master Agreement	ICSI	ECHO	Chase Tokyo
Type of Netting:					
- bilateral	x	x	x		
- multilateral				x	x
Type of Contract:					
- spot & forward	x		x	x	
- swaps		x			
- payments					x
Currencies:					
- single currency					x
- multi currency	x	x	x	x	(U.S. $)
Legal Nature:					
- position					
- netting by novation	x		x	x	
- substitution					
- open offer				x	
- master agreement	x	x	x	x	x
- close-out clause	x	x	x	x	
Parties:					
- type	banks	all parties	all parties	banks	banks
- number	+/- 40	+/- 200	9	+/- 14	+/- 200
Location/Area of operation:	London; Hong Kong; Los Angeles; New York; Singapore; Tokyo	global	North America	London; OECD countries	Tokyo; New York
Year of Introduction:	1987	1987	1992	1995	around 1950

Source: Claudio Borio and Paul Van den Bergh, *The Nature and Management of Payment System Risks: An International Perspective*, Bank for International Settlements Economic Papers, no. 36, Basle: Bank for International Settlements, February 1993. Used by permission of the Bank for International Settlements.

currently preparing the establishment of a multilateral netting system.[1] Another famous bilateral netting scheme is based on a standard master agreement drawn up by the International Swap Dealers Association (ISDA). Its major advantage is the reduction of credit risks on outstanding obligations, but it also offers the service of netting settlement flows connected with the contracts.

Furthermore, there is the International Clearing Systems Incorporation (ICSI), which is a subsidiary of Options Clearing Corporations (OCC) and was launched in June 1992. When first introduced, ICSI served eight Canadian and U.S. financial intermediaries and is limited to bilateral netting. There are, however, plans to upgrade the system to allow for multilateral netting and to get a foothold in Europe. An organization that already offers both bilateral and multilateral netting services is the North American Clearing House Organization (NACHO). It is based in the United States and groups Canadian and U.S. banks. Closely related to NACHO is the European Clearing House Organization (ECHO). Its structure allows for multilateral netting by novation and substitution for forex contracts and is domiciled in London. Its membership is essentially limited to "decently" rated financial intermediaries of the OECD countries (i.e., minimum long-term credit rating of BBB+) and some twenty-four currencies (including the ECU). Finally, there is the U.S. dollar clearing system of Chase Manhattan Bank in Tokyo. It is believed that this scheme handles about 90 percent of all forex trades denominated in U.S. dollars in Japan. Normally, correspondent customers of Chase Tokyo send and receive payment instructions during Tokyo business hours, which result in their accounts being credited or debited at Chase throughout the day. At the end of the respective business day in Tokyo, the customers are informed of their account positions. Credit balances are then withdrawn by informing Chase Tokyo to transfer part or all of the funds to New York during normal U.S business hours. Debits, on the other hand, are covered later in New York during North American business hours. Thus, even though this scheme shows some typical attributes of netting systems, it does not reduce the Herstatt risk—one payment of the forex deal is settled, while the other side still needs to be performed.

CROSS-BORDER NETTING SCHEMES AND THE REGULATORS

Netting schemes do not enjoy acceptance across the board. The argument is that the global payment system has been rendered highly fragmented and unstable by various private arrangements, which lack clear legal rules and procedures for clearing and settlement. In contrast to the domestic realm, where a sole supervisor has the authority to intervene, the international realm is basically based on bilateral

---

1. For more detail, see Hartmann (1991: 34–38); and Borio and Van den Bergh (1993: 58–59).

Table 4.4
Minimum Standards for Cross-border Netting Schemes Proposed by the Committee on Interbank Netting Schemes of the Central Banks of the Group of Ten

I.   Netting schemes should have a well-founded legal basis under all relevant jurisdictions.

II. Netting schemes participants should have a clear understanding of the impact of the particular scheme on each of the financial risks affected by the netting process.

III. Multilateral netting systems should have clearly defined procedures for the management of credit risks and liquidity risks that specify the respective responsibilities of the netting provider and the participants. These procedures should also ensure that all parties have both the incentives and the capabilities to manage and contain each of the risks they bear and that limits are placed on the maximum level of credit exposure that can be produced by each participant.

IV. Multilateral netting schemes should, at a minimum, be capable of ensuring the timely completion of daily settlements in the event of an inability to settle by the participant with the largest single net-debit position.

V.   Multilateral netting systems should have objective and publicly disclosed criteria for admission that permit fair and open access.

VI. All netting schemes should ensure the operational reliability of technical systems and the availability of backup facilities capable of completing daily processing requirements.

Source: Bank for International Settlements, *Report of the Committee on Interbank Netting Schemes of the Central Banks of the Group of Ten Countries*. Basle: Bank for International Settlements, 1990. Used by permission of the Bank for International Settlements.

or multilateral agreements whose legal enforceability depends on the netting providers' base. In other words, netting schemes are said to lack supervisory authority to operate outside the jurisdiction of home central banks (i.e., outside public monitoring and control), and to miss a lender of last resort role. Furthermore, it is argued that payment systems may create externalities that could reduce the incentives for transnational financial intermediaries to provide the necessary resources to improve the infrastructure. Finally, the tremendous growth—and profitability—has supposedly disguised the "weak" spots of payment systems. As soon as competition gets fiercer and margins smaller individual operators might no longer have an interest in upgrading the payment infrastructure.

While all these concerns should be heeded, such worries nonetheless fail to acknowledge that companies, which are competitors in daily life, can very much cooperate and act in line with generally agreed upon conventions. This argument is not intrinsically inconsistent, because intervening institutions in an environment lacking an overarching authority are *not* ineffective. As Ohmae correctly says, companies are very much able to do "what leaders of nations have always known: In a complex, uncertain world filled with dangerous opponents, it is better not to go it alone" (Ohmae, 1992: 141).

Nevertheless, as central bankers share their interest in limiting the level of systemic risks in the global financial system, most of them have been sympathetic to the idea of making improvements in the efficiency and stability of payment systems by financial intermediaries. It is in particular the cross-border netting schemes in the forex markets that caught the imagination of the regulators (Table 4.3). It has been acknowledged that netting schemes help increase the efficiency of payment systems and reduce settlement costs with the exploding forex volume by reducing the number as well as the total value of payments. Furthermore, netting schemes have been said to reduce the size of credit and liquidity exposures and thereby contain systemic risks. The benevolent treatment of private cross-border netting schemes by the regulators (Table 4.4) is revealed not the least by the two reports published by the BIS on this topic (1989, 1990).

Thus, it is safe to conclude that netting schemes are not just a fad, but are relevant features of international relations. In fact, netting schemes are just about to replace the traditional correspondent services of domestic clearing and settlement systems where cross-border trading activities are involved. Even though payments in a given currency are ultimately settled through the accounts of the respective central bank, global financial operators are creating truly transnational settlement systems, separating clearing processes from the final settlement.

5

Conclusion

Have we come to the end of the 300-year-old attempt to regulate and stabilize money, on which, after all, both the nation-state and the international system are largely based?

— Peter Drucker

This study is basically confined to the theoretical and conceptual aspects of global affairs, emphasizing processes and structures and borrowing heavily from microeconomics and its neoclassical microtheory. It shows that certain nonstate actors have become independent agents of change and therefore should be included in any analysis of international relations. It also proves that the theory of transnational regimes, including nonstructural systemic factors determining nonstate strategies (nonstructural stimuli for nonstate actors' behavior and their capability to cooperate and communicate), is a highly relevant tool for a theoretically informed analysis of the new global system.

Despite the emphasis on paradigmatic, ontological, and epistemological aspects, the connection to reality has been achieved through empirical evidence in the form of historical events. The study affirmatively answers the question whether transnational regimes influence individual actors: in all mentioned cases it is possible to witness a modified behavior on the part of the regime participants. These modifications naturally differ in intensity, depending on the area and interest of individual actors, but it is possible to observe modifications of behavior toward the regimes' goals. In this sense, transnational regimes are both politically and materially effective. Critics may here object by arguing that the regimes' necessity and sufficiency still need to be proven. However, transnational regimes are not only necessary (given the complexity of global finance and the danger of systemic crises), but also sufficient. Sometimes critics confuse effectiveness with quality, and therefore overlook the fact that regimes are useful instruments for achieving transnational cooperation by channeling actor behavior in a certain direction. The "civilization" of global finance should, however, not lead to the conclusion that the concentration and institutionalization of global affairs are imminent; cooperation may break down or transnational regimes may fall apart. This is because the problems, which are to be overcome by transnational regimes, are themselves products of human activity. Nonetheless, transnational regimes offer ways to encourage the emergence of order and stability in global affairs.

Regardless of its significance, the criticisms that might be voiced against the theory of transnational regimes should be heeded. It is especially the theory's uneasy relationship with ideas and knowledge and its difficulty endorsing the basic arguments of knowledge-based concepts that need attention. The theory of transnational regimes therefore falls short of the high aspiration of some theorists of international relations who expect theories to combine "*historical* understanding, *substantive* explanation, *totalizing* theory, and a *moral* vocation of reason" (Rosenberg, 1994: 85).

IMPLICATIONS

The ontology professed in this book obviously colludes with that held by realists who belittle the importance of nonstate actors in world finance. Underhill, for instance, maintains that it is the political realm that "shapes the institutional context of international capital markets" (Underhill, 1991: 197), and that "politics, through the medium of state decision-making, continues to determine the pattern of development" (ibid.: 200). Underhill is certainly correct when he argues that "the emergence of financial markets in the international domain does not represent the spontaneous pattern of economics textbooks" (Underhill, 1993: 4) but is a result of political decisions or nondecisions. Nonetheless, the argument that states have established the rules and therefore can change the name of the game at any given time is overly naive, given the high opportunity costs of withdrawing from the global market. The predominance of states in global affairs can therefore not be taken for granted any longer. New actors have entered the scene and need to be accounted for. Their actions cannot be taken as epiphenomenal, but have to be regarded as influential forces impacting the social world.

Against this background, transnational regime theory makes not only the case for a reopening of the debate on cosmopolitanism, but also directs attention to a new way of structuring the global system. In so doing, it also offers a convincing policy prescription to help overcome the management problems in global finance by building "islands of order in a sea of anarchy" (Donnelly, 1986: 601). As nonstate actors can perform important political functions and are able to cooperate, transnational institutions become a realistic option for areas that states have voluntarily vacated, such as the foreign exchange markets, cross-border payment systems (e.g., netting), or human rights (e.g., International Committee of the Red Cross or Amnesty International) and for areas where a public response is too expensive.

All in all, transnational regime theory enriches the ontology of the international political economy and offers an interesting policy mix that could change the way of thinking about global affairs and thus the structure of the globe.

Appendix 1: What Are Systemic Risks?

For many observers of the global financial market, crises in the financial realm seem to have occurred more frequently since the 1980s than in earlier periods. This has led to an increased interest in the research of the causes of financial crises and their impact on systemic stability. But how can financial crises and their consequences be best characterized? To begin with, it is beneficial to distinguish between two interlinked terms: systemic crisis and systemic risk. Financial systemic crises are disturbances that spread from the financial realm to other realms of the economic system. This is true not only when a financial system completely collapses with macroeconomic consequences, but also when disturbances economically call for the intervention of market participants or regulators. Systemic risk, on the other hand, measures only the probability of such a crisis occurring. There are basically two (macroeconomic) approaches to the causes of financial crises: the monetarist and the financial-fragility approach.

The latter is one of the oldest economic theories of systemic crises. It was originally formulated by Fisher (1932, 1933) and was later refined by Minsky (1972, 1982) and Kindleberger (1978). According to its defenders, there are a number of reasons for systemic risks: rising debt load during an economic upswing, decreasing liquidity of corporate and financial intermediaries, and a changing institutional and regulatory environment. In other words, political and macroeconomic changes ameliorate the environment in which the economy makes investment decisions. The resulting optimism then translates into higher prices of investment and finished goods, making it easier to borrow. Higher prices (i.e., inflation) then also reduce the real value of financial obligations, thus increasing the willingness to take out more loans—a spiral that is further supported by the sped-up money circulation. Eventually, nominal interest rates rise so much that debtors begin to refinance their debts short term. Intensified competition among financial intermediaries then leads to more credits with lower margins. As a result, certain industries are overindebted so that a liquidity problem occurs. When all market participants begin to realize the danger in which the financial system is, mass liquidation of assets is likely to occur, further fueled by credit rationings or cancellations of credit lines, and thus could cause a systemic crisis. In Flanders' lucid language,

> a credit boom results in excess borrowing on the basis of over-inflated estimates of current and future wealth. When the bubble eventually bursts, falling asset prices and the slowing of economic activity makes these debt burdens harder to sustain. Indebted companies and individuals have to cut down their investment and consumption to pay off debt, thus depressing activity further. The danger in this situation is that asset prices deflation and over-indebtedness will feed on one another in a debt-deflationary spiral. As asset prices fall, and real interest rates rise, more and more companies may be forced into liquidating their debts, leading to more price falls, and further depressing economic activity. Eventually . . . lower bank deposits and bank failures cause the deflationary virus to spread through the economy, meaning a collapse in confidence and all-out depression. (Flanders, 1995: 21)

For the monetarist school, on the other hand, financial crises are created by banking panics that result from growing concern about some banking groups' solvency (Friedman and Schwartz, 1963; Schwartz, 1986). That is, if depositors have reason to believe that their banks are riskier than before, they will suddenly demand redemption of their deposits. Faced with a "run" of deposit withdrawals, banks would be forced to suspend convertibility of their debt into cash. The ensuing monetary squeeze would then cause economic disturbances and, depending on the intensity of the bank run, a contraction in the production sector, thereby causing a systemic crisis. Such a national crisis could easily be transmitted internationally if fixed exchange rate systems are in place. That is why monetarists come out against such systems. The monetarist policy prescription involves a stable and predictable path to money supply (i.e., conservative monetary policy), but foresees a money supply expansion in the case of a crisis (Davis, 1995: 131). Deposit insurance or a lender of last resort can help avoid the occurrence of bank runs or panics. Even though most banking panics are actually caused by a confidence crisis, the event that forces banks to close their doors is their inability to continue paying out their customers. This is likely when a significant number of banks are suddenly and unexpectedly forced by their customers to convert deposits into currency.

Even though the financial-fragility and the monetarist approaches are the most famous and widely cited economic theories of systemic risk, there are nonetheless other approaches that also try to explain how financial instability is triggered. Most of them, such as the asymmetric information and agency cost or the credit rationing approach, do not seek to substitute but to complement the two macroapproaches. In fact, both credit rationing and agency costs illustrate how macroeconomic crises are transmitted through the financial system. Regardless of the strengths and weaknesses of these economic theories of financial crises, they all have the same policy implication. In order to protect retail investors and prevent systemic risks, these theories come out in favor of public regulation. The argument is that banks in a world lacking regulation often experience bank runs and that systemic collapses occur at regular intervals. Only large amounts of capital would allow banks to cope with a possible financial squeeze. A large capital base makes banking, however, extremely expensive and thus unprofitable. Therefore, regulators argue, that it is necessary to introduce a lender of last resort and a deposit insurance.

Basle Committee) and comprised representatives of the central banks and banking regulatory agencies of the Group of Ten, including Luxembourg and Switzerland. As the Committee is neither an international nor a supranational body, it cannot make any binding resolutions but can only make recommendations. These recommendations may subsequently be implemented in national legislation by the relevant national banking regulatory agency. Originally, the Committee was supposed to develop early warning systems for the international financial markets, but since the formation of the Committee this goal has increasingly shifted toward bridging gaps in the supervisory network and achieving a worldwide improvement in the scope and quality of banking regulation. The result was the 1975 Concordat setting out the principles that no foreign bank can be allowed to avoid supervision and that supervision must be appropriate. This implied that bank supervision had to be elevated to the multilateral level.

In 1982 Italy's largest bank, Banco Ambrosiano, ran into difficulties as a result of overdue foreign loans. The Italian authorities refused to accept responsibility for foreign subsidiaries of the bank, demonstrating a need to revise the 1975 Concordat. The main point in the revision which took place in 1983 was the recommendation that a transnationally active banking group should always be treated as such on a consolidated basis by a supervisory authority (BIS, 1983). Supervision of the entire group would be carried out by the supervisory authority responsible for the headquarters of the parent company, while the examination of the financial solidity of subsidiaries or branches would be the responsibility of the local supervisory authorities. Branches of foreign banks would be licensed only if the group were subject to appropriate consolidated supervision, and bank regulators should prevent their own banks from becoming active in countries where legislation did not permit consolidated supervision. The Bank of Credit and Commerce International (BCCI) scandal of 1991 put the issue of country of origin control back in the spotlight.

The next major step came in 1988, when the so-called Basle Accord was published (BIS, 1988). It covered appropriate capital standards for financial intermediaries and introduced risk-weighted capital standards on a global stage in place of the fixed capital-to-asset ratios. This was necessary because the fixed capital-to-asset ratio did not distinguish between good and bad asset quality nor include off-balance-sheet items. Since then, the Basle Accord was amended and revised on a number of occasions (BIS, 1991, 1993).

In the 1990s, the focus of interest moved on to market risks. The BIS launched a package of new consultative papers. The most important consequences were approval for taking into account correlations when calculating risk exposure and the acceptance of in-house risk measurement models (BIS, 1995a). The explosive growth of derivatives in recent years has also led to explicit calls for more intensive regulation of this market segment. Following a series of losses due to lack of

Appendix 2: The BIS and Supervision

Since 1974, when the Bank for International Settlements (BIS) established the so-called Cooke Committee as a result of the collapse of three banks (Herstatt Bank in Germany, Franklin National Bank in New York, the British-Israeli Bank in London), it has assumed an important role in the supervision of financial intermediaries.[1] In contrast to the liberalization efforts of the World Trade Organization (WTO) and the Organization for Economic Cooperation and Development (OECD) the aim is not primarily deregulation but rather appropriate and, in particular, up-to-the-minute monitoring of risks in global banking. The means used are the exchange of information and cooperation between the national regulatory agencies and the setting of minimum standards in the form of recommendations to the regulatory authorities in member states.

Clearly, the reason for the increased importance of the BIS was the internationalization of private finance which created new risks. As financial intermediaries started to give their balance sheets an international flavor on both the assets and the liabilities side, the scope and effectiveness of domestic bank regulation became limited. The internationalization also increased the vulnerability of domestic financial markets to the liquidity and solvency problems of foreign banks. In response, the central bank governors of the G-10 states asked Peter Cooke of the Bank of England to start work on forming a BIS committee to supervise transnationally active financial intermediaries that became known as the Cooke Committee (or

---

1. For a more detailed account of the history of the BIS, see Kapstein (1991).

Basle Committee) and comprised representatives of the central banks and banking regulatory agencies of the Group of Ten, including Luxembourg and Switzerland. As the Committee is neither an international nor a supranational body, it cannot make any binding resolutions but can only make recommendations. These recommendations may subsequently be implemented in national legislation by the relevant national banking regulatory agency. Originally, the Committee was supposed to develop early warning systems for the international financial markets, but since the formation of the Committee this goal has increasingly shifted toward bridging gaps in the supervisory network and achieving a worldwide improvement in the scope and quality of banking regulation. The result was the 1975 Concordat setting out the principles that no foreign bank can be allowed to avoid supervision and that supervision must be appropriate. This implied that bank supervision had to be elevated to the multilateral level.

In 1982 Italy's largest bank, Banco Ambrosiano, ran into difficulties as a result of overdue foreign loans. The Italian authorities refused to accept responsibility for foreign subsidiaries of the bank, demonstrating a need to revise the 1975 Concordat. The main point in the revision which took place in 1983 was the recommendation that a transnationally active banking group should always be treated as such on a consolidated basis by a supervisory authority (BIS, 1983). Supervision of the entire group would be carried out by the supervisory authority responsible for the headquarters of the parent company, while the examination of the financial solidity of subsidiaries or branches would be the responsibility of the local supervisory authorities. Branches of foreign banks would be licensed only if the group were subject to appropriate consolidated supervision, and bank regulators should prevent their own banks from becoming active in countries where legislation did not permit consolidated supervision. The Bank of Credit and Commerce International (BCCI) scandal of 1991 put the issue of country of origin control back in the spotlight.

The next major step came in 1988, when the so-called Basle Accord was published (BIS, 1988). It covered appropriate capital standards for financial intermediaries and introduced risk-weighted capital standards on a global stage in place of the fixed capital-to-asset ratios. This was necessary because the fixed capital-to-asset ratio did not distinguish between good and bad asset quality nor include off-balance-sheet items. Since then, the Basle Accord was amended and revised on a number of occasions (BIS, 1991, 1993).

In the 1990s, the focus of interest moved on to market risks. The BIS launched a package of new consultative papers. The most important consequences were approval for taking into account correlations when calculating risk exposure and the acceptance of in-house risk measurement models (BIS, 1995a). The explosive growth of derivatives in recent years has also led to explicit calls for more intensive regulation of this market segment. Following a series of losses due to lack of approach, do not seek to substitute but to complement the two macroapproaches. In fact, both credit rationing and agency costs illustrate how macroeconomic crises are transmitted through the financial system. Regardless of the strengths and weaknesses of these economic theories of financial crises, they all have the same policy implication. In order to protect retail investors and prevent systemic risks, these theories come out in favor of public regulation. The argument is that banks in a world lacking regulation often experience bank runs and that systemic collapses occur at regular intervals. Only large amounts of capital would allow banks to cope with a possible financial squeeze. A large capital base makes banking, however, extremely expensive and thus unprofitable. Therefore, regulators argue, that it is necessary to introduce a lender of last resort and a deposit insurance.

knowhow and inadequate supervision of derivatives activities the Cooke Committee produced a number of new publications. Official efforts to improve market transparency took concrete form in a February 1995 report by the central banks of the G-10 countries (BIS, 1995b). This report detailed the data required to facilitate supervision of the derivatives market and contained proposals for coordinated production and dissemination of statistics by the central banks. As the first concrete step, in April 1995 a broad-based survey of derivatives business was carried out in 26 countries, along with the regular triennial survey of central banks on forex futures. Following the failure of Barings in February 1995 the securities supervisory agencies in 16 countries announced measures in May 1995 to strengthen supervision of the futures exchanges and to improve the flow of information between the markets. For its part, the Basle Committee presented joint proposals with the International Organization of Securities Commissions (IOSCO) with the goal of collecting aggregate market data on the derivatives activities of banks at regular intervals (BIS, 1995c).

On the initiative of the Basle Committee an informal group was formed in 1993 of banking, insurance and securities regulators ("Tripartite Group") to look at the problems of supervising financial conglomerates. In response to the globalization of financial markets, financial conglomerates are frequently formed from transnationally active companies. International coordination of supervision is further complicated by differing financial and supervisory systems in individual countries. In its informal discussion paper, the Tripartite Group presented possible solutions to appropriate supervision of such financial conglomerates (BIS, 1995d). The Group's considerations center on the improvement of the transparency of organizational and management structures, the avoidance of knock-on risks, and the prevention of multiple employment of capital base.

The trend toward the formation of financial conglomerates has accelerated in recent years. This necessitated intensified cooperation among the various supervisory authorities supplemented by supervision on a consolidated basis ("Solo-Plus" supervision). The Basle Committee, IOSCO, and the International Association of Insurance Supervisors (IAIS) have agreed to set up a joint forum to develop some practical proposals.

What shape will future regulation and supervision take? International harmonization of supervision will certainly become more important. There are signs that it is no longer enough for the supervisory agencies to act in concert: the appearance of transnationally active financial conglomerates in different sectors makes the task of identifying potential risks posed by this form of organization increasingly more difficult and complicated. In future, cooperation will be needed at the international level among the supervisory agencies for the various financial sectors. This will make heavy demands in terms of cooperation and the coordination of the activities of supervisors. Regarding regulation it will become necessary to find an optimal intensity of regulation that neither restricts the scope for innovation nor stifles the flexibility of financial intermediaries in responding to changing conditions. In fact, financial operators are often quicker and more efficient in tackling the different challenges in the global financial market, as the London Club or the private netting arrangements have shown. This suggests that financial intermediaries and their institutions should be included in the global regulatory system.

Appendix 3: The EMS Crises of 1992–93

Forex speculators make easy scapegoats for public regulatory bodies. Everytime there are turbulences in the forex markets, traders are being blamed. However, the real culprits are often the governments themselves. This can be shown nicely against the background of the exit of the pound and the lira from the European Exchange Rate Mechanism[1] (ERM) in September 1992 and the virtual collapse of the system in August 1993 when virtually all currency bands were widened to 15 percent.

Why did the ERM erupt after 15 years of relative calm? Essentially, the European governments failed to coordinate their domestic policies and to realize that the ERM was prone to external economic shocks. So it came that most European currencies which had to be kept within narrow bands of 2.25 percent around their central rates except for the Portuguese escudo and the Spanish peseta that were allowed to move

---

1. The ERM is one of the key features of the EMS (European Monetary System). Among the others are exchange realignments, the European Currency Unit (ECU), central rates, limited exchange rate margins of fluctuation, central bank interventions, divergence indicators, the European Monetary Cooperation Fund (EMCF), and credit facilities. According to the Maastricht Treaty, the EMS is to be replaced by the European single currency (euro) by 1 January 1999. For those countries that do not initially meet the five qualifying criteria (inflation, interest rates, budget deficit, long-term government debt, EMS membership) and therefore cannot participate from the beginning, there will be an EMS II, binding their national currencies to the euro.

within a band of 6 percent were able to move up to 15 percent from their respective central rates. In fact, the only exchange rate which was kept to its old band was the D-mark/Dutch guilder rate.[1] What went wrong? There are basically two reasons. One was the diverging domestic policies that emerged after Germany's reunification. The second was the considerable doubts about the ratification of the Maastricht Treaty. When Germany decided to introduce the one for one parity of ostmark to D-mark (DM) and failed to keep firm control on its fiscal policy to finance its reunification, a shock wave hit the ERM. These measures led to high interest rates in Germany due to heavy borrowing, exactly at a time when the rest of Europe needed low rates. That is to say, Germany went from a budget surplus in the year preceding reunification to a deficit after integration, accompanied by a change in the trade balance of Germany from a current account surplus before 1990 into a deficit after reunification. Clearly, this combination put pressure on the German government to let its currency be revalued (appreciated) against the currencies of Germany's major European trading partners.[2] It was argued that the real appreciation would result in a current account deficit—the logical counterpart to the import of foreign capital to be able to finance reunification.[3]

The German government was well aware of the need to realign the EMS parities. Indeed, it proposed to its trading partners to agree on an appreciation of the D-mark. Yet Germany's endeavors were not crowned with success; its partners showed no intention of devaluing their currencies against the DM. The most ardent defender of the status quo was France, which feared that its strong French franc policy—the key element of its domestic economic policy—would be jeopardized by a devalued franc. In light of the failed general realignment of nominal rates the only remaining alternative to achieve the increase in the real forex rate for the DM was for Germany to have its inflation rate exceed that of its trading partners. That is exactly what

1. Members of the ERM are required to intervene in the forex markets in *unlimited* amounts in order to prevent their respective currencies from breaking through the limits fixed in the parity grid. For instance, if a currency appreciates to its maximum level against one or several of the other members' currencies, the respective central bank is obliged to buy weak currencies and sell the strong ones. Since the 1987 Basle-Nyborg Agreement, members were encouraged to tame currency fluctuations not through interventions, but through interest rates movements.

2. At the same time when Germany was running a deficit, the United States was fighting against deflation by keeping its interest rates at low levels. This factor led to an outflow of funds from the United States into Germany, thus adding to the upward pressure on the D-mark.

3. The central point of international payments is that if a country is running a current account deficit (receiving less from sales to foreign countries than it spends abroad) the deficit needs to be financed by selling assets or borrowing abroad. Thus: Current Account Deficit + Net Capital Inflow = 0.

happened following the reunification act which was partly a product of the expansionary fiscal policy and partly of the increased monetary growth resulting from monetary unification ("one for one parity").

The conservative Bundesbank responded as usual by embarking on a restrictive monetary policy which inevitably caused German interest to soar dramatically, at a time when the other EMS members needed low interest rates. Understandably, Germany's partners were increasingly concerned about the commencing recession in their domestic economies. In order to keep the forex parities stable, these countries were, however, left with little else than to maintain their interest rates at some higher level than was necessary from a purely domestic economic viewpoint. This scenario was exactly the stuff governments' nightmares are made of. The diverging policies followed by the Bundesbank and the other EMS members respectively, made many financial market operators question whether the EMS members would be willing and able to defend their respective forex rates in view of high interest rates. These concerns surely led to an increased vulnerability of the ERM.

At the same time when the EMS partners could not agree on policy convergence, another factor threatened the laid down parities of the EMS: the Maastricht Treaty. According to the Treaty's paragraphs, it needed unanimity to come into force. But the Danish rejection of the Treaty's provisions in June 1992 in a referendum put a big question mark behind the whole idea of monetary union. In addition, popular feelings in France in favor of the Maastricht Treaty dangerously shifted, thus threatening to turn down the referendum called by President Mitterrand in September of the same year. The story plot suggested that a devaluation of overvalued currencies would be very much likely.

The most vulnerable candidates were those unfortunate EMS members with currencies that witnessed deteriorating competitiveness resulting from high inflation after the 1987 EMS realignment. Italy, for instance, saw its consumer prices rise by more than 30 percent since 1987, compared to only about 15 percent in France. The ensuing real appreciation of the lira stirred up anxieties over a "lasting" huge current account deficit for Italy. As a result, investors, increasingly uneasy about the imminent threat of devaluation, began to sell their Italian assets, thereby adding to the downward trend of the Italian currency. Intensified by forex dealers betting on a devaluation, this pressure was eventually too much for the Italian central bank to bear so that it eventually decided to withdraw the lira from the ERM in September 1992. In fact, neither heavy interventions nor an increase of the discount rate could prevent the lira's devaluation. The Pound sterling (the United Kingdom has been an ERM member only since 1990) experienced the same fate. As in the case of the lira, global investors concluded that the British currency was overvalued and began to sell their sterling denominated assets. Overwhelmed by the market power, the British government was forced to suspend the pound's membership in the ERM. The vulnerability of overvalued European currencies, revealed by the exit of the lira and pound, had naturally not gone unnoticed. Financial intermediaries began to shift their assets away from weak currencies into strong currencies, and by May 1993, Ireland, Portugal, and Spain had to let their currencies be depreciated against those currencies of the other ERM members, which was the first step of the ERM crisis.

The second blow to the system came in August 1993, when in light of the ongoing recession in Europe, popular support for a high interests policy to keep forex rates stable slowly but surely eroded. Indeed, the EMS members were caught in a predicament since they could keep their currencies unchanged only when the Bundesbank eased its tight policy. Otherwise they would have to devalue in order to circumvent pressures on their domestic economies. Again, financial operators started to bet that the clash between domestic policy priorities and macroeconomic policy coordination would be won by domestic considerations. So it came that when the German central bankers failed to lower the discount rate on 29 July 1993, a massive exodus from supposedly overvalued currencies ensued, leaving EC ministers at their shortly convened emergency meeting with little else than to take notice of the fait accompli. As a result, the European currencies remaining in the ERM were allowed to fluctuate within a band regime of 15 percent.[1]

This event sent regulators and academics alike back to the drawing board. Policymakers in particular were adopting the view that it was the totally irresponsible gamblers and their gigantic global casino that brought down the ERM. Even though it comes in handy for governments to blame the reckless speculators for their own wrongdoings, it was the governments themselves that established a monetary environment which they now are unable to control. That is, a system in which forex market participants reward sound monetary and fiscal policies and unmercifully force changes on inflationary ones. They did so, to compound the pressures on them, by allowing capital to flow freely around the world. Therefore, the official policies have to be blamed when financial markets turn "chaotic." In fact, attacks on strong currencies can easily backfire, as the Austrian case in August 1993 nicely showed when traders were forced to cover their short positions at a loss.

The above story plot explicitly proves that it would be wrong to blame forex speculators. In fact, by pointing to alternative steps which could have prevented the crisis from developing, it is possible to show that it was actually a product of the

---

1. It is noteworthy that the European central banks were anything but sad about the crisis that resulted in the conversion of the EMS into a de facto floating exchange rate system. On the contrary, they hoped the breakdown would allow them to exploit the newly found flexibility in formulating independent monetary policies.

states' unwillingness to coordinate their policies that brought down the EMS regime. Italy and Great Britain, for instance, could have lowered their inflation rates much earlier. France, on the other hand, could have adopted the German idea of a realignment to manage the macroeconomic asymmetries emerging after the German reunification. And the German authorities should have checked their expansionary fiscal policies, thus controlling the inflationary effects much better. Moreover, it should have paid more attention to the domestic needs of their fellow partners by lowering its interest rates much sooner and more quickly.

Glossary

Bank for International Settlements (BIS): The world's oldest international currency organization. It was founded on 20 January 1930 at the Hague Conference in connection with handling the payment of reparations by the German Reich from the First World War. The founders were the presidents of the central banks of Belgium, France, Germany, Italy, Japan, and the United Kingdom as well as the representatives of a U.S. banking group. Today, it functions as the "central bank for central banks."

Bardepot: A German law that requires a certain percentage of foreign borrowings by German residents to be placed in cash in a non-interest-bearing account with the Bundesbank.

Basis Point: 1/100 of one percent (i.e., 0.01%).

Basle Agreements: Accords among the G-10 countries to harmonize banking supervision (i.e., minimum standards of prudential supervision). Normally, they refer to the so-called agreement on capital adequacy.

Brady Bond: Paper issued by governments in exchange for restructured commercial bank debt.

Capital Adequacy: Regulatory requirements for financial intermediaries to maintain a certain ratio of total equity to assets.

City: The City of London, the financial center of the United Kingdom.

Clearing House: An organization that registers, monitors, matches, and guarantees deals and executes the financial settlement of those transactions.

Clearing System: A transaction system established to expedite settlements.

Counterparty Risk: The risk that one party of a deal will go bankrupt before the deal is completed.

Credit Rationing: Limited provision of debt to a borrower.

Credit Risk: The risk that a party will default on its obligations prior to maturity.

Cross Default: A covenant by an issuer stating that if there is a default in a payment under its other borrowings, such nonpayment will be considered an event of default in respect of the issue to which the cross default covenant applies.

Debt-Service Ratio: Costs of paying principal and interest payments on debt relative to exports. A level of 20 to 25 percent is considered acceptable.

Default: The failure to fulfill the conditions of a contract.

Deregulation: The relaxation of regulations concerning a certain market.

Economic Efficiency: A situation in which no actor can be made better off without somebody else being made worse off (Pareto-optimum).

Exchange Controls: Government control of gold and forex trading. (Control, however, applies only to residents because it is too complicated for governments to control the activities of nonresidents as well).

Externalities: Welfare costs that are not fully internalized by the market.

Financial Conglomerates (also known as "Allfinanz" or "bancassurance"): Groups of affiliated companies under central management whose activities involve primarily offering various financial services in at least two different financial sectors (banking, securities, insurance).

Financial Fragility: A state of increased vulnerability to default of households, corporates, and financial intermediaries. *See also* systemic risk.

Financial Intermediaries: Companies that make loans or other investments.

Group of Ten (G-10): Belgium, Canada, France, Germany, Italy, the Netherlands, Sweden, Switzerland, the United Kingdom, and the United States. These countries are members of the board of directors, i.e. the group of experts or board of central bank governors. Legally speaking, however, the membership actually includes all BIS shareholders.

Hedging: Reducing risks on a position.

Insolvency: A situation when liabilities exceed assets on a balance sheet of a financial intermediary.

Interest Equalization Tax (IET): Tax of up to fifteen percent used in the United States between 1963–74 on many foreign securities.

International Bank Credit Analyst (IBCA): Credit rating agency assessing financial actors.

International Organization of Securities Commissions (IOSCO): Association of those responsible for regulating securities dealing in over fifty member states. Its goal is to set uniform standards and to promote the free exchange of information on member states' financial markets. The organization consists of various committees, with the Technical Committee regarded as one of the most influential.

International Securities Market Association (ISMA): Organization for the international securities market. It acts as the market regulatory agent.

Invisible Hand: Adam Smith's metaphor of the market. He argued that individuals who pursue their own goals will unintentionally contribute to the general welfare.

Liquidity Risk: The risk that a party will settle its obligation not on maturity date, but on a date thereafter.

London Club: Informal cooperation between financial intermediaries serving as a forum to deal with restructuring deals concerning sovereign debt. *See also* Paris Club.

London Interbank Offered Rate ("LIBOR"): The rate at which prime banks offer to make Eurocurrency deposits with other prime banks for a given maturity in London.

Market Failure: A situation in which imperfections in the market system impair the efficient use of the employed resources. *See also* economic efficiency.

Market Risk: The risk that the market price of a security is changing while an investor is holding a position in it.

MATIF (Marché à Terme International de France): A Paris-based market for derivatives products.

Monetarism: A school in economics assuming that business cycles, employment, inflation, etc. are a function of money supply rather than fiscal policy.

Moody's: Credit rating agency assessing corporate and sovereign debt.

Netting by Close-out: An arrangement to settle all but not yet mature obligations by one single payment upon the occurrence of previously defined events.

Netting by Novation: The replacement of two deals between two parties by one single deal, thus satisfying and discharging the original deals.

Novation and Substitution: The procedure that changes the deal between two parties such that a third party is involved as an intermediary creditor or debtor. The deal is then novated, thus satisfying and discharging the original deal.

Off-balance Sheet Liabilities: Corporate obligations that are not shown on the balance sheet.

Opportunity Costs: The costs incurred by failing to employ resources in the most profitable alternative activity.

OTC (over-the-counter) Market: An exchange market that is not organized in an exchange.

Pari Passu: Term used in the context of unsecured debt securities that are said to rank equally with each other or with other unsecured debt.

Paris Club: Cooperation between creditor countries that serves as a forum to deal with restructuring deals concerning sovereign debt. *See also* London Club.

Position Netting: The netting of payment instructions with respect to obligations between two or more parties, but which neither satisfies nor discharges the original obligations.

Primary Market: A market in which financial claims are issued. *See also* secondary market.

Rational Expectation: A hypothesis that a party behaves in light of all the available information; that is, the individual's expectations do not contain any systematic errors.

Realism: Paradigm in international relations that holds that states are the most important actors in world politics and that peace is maintained only by the balance of power. Military might and economic power define the state ranking.

Regulation: Rules that define the permissible activities of financial intermediaries.

Samurai Bond: A foreign bond issued in Japan.

Secondary Market: The market for securities and loans that is provided by market-makers between the deal-making and its maturity.

Settlement Date: The date a transaction is cleared; that is, payment is effected and securities are delivered.

Settlement Risk: The risk that a party will default on one or more of its obligations to its counterparties.

Soft Loan: A loan with an artificially low interest rate. Soft loans are often made to developing countries by the industrialized countries for political or ideological purposes.

Sovereign Risk: Risk of lending to countries.

Special Drawing Rights (SDR): IMF currency unit.

Standard and Poor's: Credit rating agency assessing corporate and sovereign debt.

State-centric Politics: *See* realism.

Supervision: Process by which financial intermediaries are checked through licensing, oversight, sanctioning, and crisis management.

Syndicated Loan: A loan by two or more banks to one borrower at a previously negotiated margin over short-term interest rates.

Systemic Risk: The risk that the inability of a party to honor its obligations on maturity date will make other participants insolvent as well. *See also* financial fragility.

Transnational Regimes: Institutions (principles, norms, rules) that regulate transnational actions within particular issue-areas.

References

Adler, Emanuel, and Peter Haas. "Conclusion: Epistemic Communities, World Order, and the Creation of a Reflective Research Program." *International Organization* 46, no. 1 (1992): 367–90.

Allison, Graham. *Essence of Decision: Explaining the Cuban Missile Crisis*. Boston: Little, Brown, 1971.

Andersen, Palle. "Economic Growth and Financial Markets: The Experience of Four Asian Countries." *The Amex Bank Review*. Finance and the International Economy, no. 7. Oxford: Oxford University Press, 1993.

Axelrod, Robert. *The Evolution of Cooperation*. New York: Basic Books, 1984.

Axelrod, Robert, and Robert Keohane. "Achieving Cooperation under Anarchy." In *Cooperation under Anarchy*, edited by Kenneth Oye. Princeton: Princeton University Press, 1986.

Ayer, A. J. *Language, Truth and Logic* [1936]. Harmondsworth: Penguin, 1990.

Bagehot, Walter. *Lombard Street* [1873]. New York: Dutton, 1921.

Bank for International Settlements. *Principles for the Supervision of Banks' Foreign Establishments ("Basle Concordat")*. Basle: Bank for International Settlements, 1983.

———. *International Convergence of Capital Measurement and Capital Standards ("Basle Accord")*. Basle: Bank for International Settlements, 1988.

———. *Report on Netting Schemes*. Basle: Bank for International Settlements, 1989.

———. *Report of the Committee on Interbank Netting Schemes of the Central Banks of the Group of Ten Countries*. Basle: Bank for International Settlements, 1990.

———. *Amendment of the Basle Capital Accord in Respect of the Inclusion of General Provisions/General Loan-Loss Reserves in Capital*. Basle: Bank for International Settlements, 1991.

————. *Delivery versus Payment in Securities Settlement Systems*. Basle: Bank for International Settlements, 1992.

————. *The Supervisory Recognition of Netting for Capital Adequacy Purposes*. Basle: Bank for International Settlements, 1993.

————. 1995a. *An Internal Model-based Approach to Market Risk Capital Requirements*. Basle: Bank for International Settlements.

————. 1995b. *Issues of Measurement Related to Market Size and Macroprudential Risks in Derivatives Markets*. Basle: Bank for International Settlements.

————. 1995c. *Framework for Supervisory Information About the Derivatives Activities of Banks and Securities Firms (Joint Report by the Basle Committee and the Technical Committee of the IOSCO)*. Basle: Bank for International Settlements.

————. 1995d. *The Supervision of Financial Conglomerates (A Report by the Tripartite Group of Bank, Securities, and Insurance Regulators)*. Basle: Bank for International Settlements.

————. *66th Annual Report*. Basle: Bank for International Settlements, 1996.

Barry, Brian, and Russell Hardin. "Individual Actions and Collective Consequences." In *Rational Man and Irrational Society: An Introduction and Sourcebook*, edited by Brian Barry and Russell Hardin, London: Sage, 1982.

Barston, Ronald. *Modern Diplomacy*. London: Longman, 1988.

Bernauer, Thomas. "The Effect of International Environmental Institutions: How We Might Learn More." *International Organization* 49, no. 2 (1995): 351–77.

Bird, Graham. *World Finance and Adjustment: An Agenda for Reform*. New York: St. Martin's, 1985.

Borio, Claudio, and Paul Van den Bergh. *The Nature and Management of Payment System Risks: An International Perspective*. Bank for International Settlements Economic Papers, no. 36. Basle: Bank for International Settlements, February 1993.

Bryant, Ralph. *International Financial Intermediation*. Washington, D.C.: Brookings Institution, 1987.

Carr, Edward Hallet. *What Is History?* [1961]. 2nd ed. Harmondsworth: Penguin, 1990.

Coase, Ronald. "The Nature of the Firm." *Economica* (1937): 386–405.

Cooke, Peter. "International Convergence of Capital Adequacy Measurement and Standards." In *The Future of Financial Systems and Service: Essays in Honour of Jack Revell*, edited by Edward Gardener. London: Macmillan, 1990.

Cooper, Richard. "The Interest Equalization Tax: An Experiment in the Separation of Capital Markets." *Finanzarchiv* 24 (1965): 447–71.

Credit Suisse First Boston. *Prospects 1995: Q2*. April 1995.

Credit Suisse Research. *Latin American Quarterly*. May 1996.

Dale, Richard. *The Regulation of International Banking*. Cambridge: Woodhead-Faulkner, 1984.

————, ed. *Financial Deregulation*. Cambridge: Woodhead-Faulkner, 1986.

————. "Stock Market Instability and Financial Regulation." In *The Future of Financial Systems and Services: Essays in Honour of Jack Revell*, edited by Edward Gardener. London: Macmillan, 1990.

————. "Just How Safe Should Banks Be?" *International Currency Review* 21, no. 4 (1992): 5–14.

Dale, Richard, and Richard Mattione. *Managing Global Debt*. Staff Paper. Washington, D.C.: Brookings Institution, 1983.

Davis, Philip. *Debt, Financial Fragility, and Systemic Risk*. Oxford: Clarendon, 1995.

De Grauwe, Paul. *International Money: Post-War Trends and Theories*. Oxford: Clarendon, 1990.

De Gregorio, José, and Pablo Guidotti. *Financial Development and Economic Growth*. International Monetary Fund Working Paper, no. 82. Washington, D.C.: International Monetary Fund, 1992.

Deutsch, Karl, et al. *Political Community and the North Atlantic Area*. Princeton: Princeton University Press, 1957.

Donnelly, Jack. "International Human Rights: A Regime Analysis." *International Organization* 40, no. 3 (1986): 599–641.

Dornbusch, Rudiger. "Expectations and Exchange Rate Dynamics." *Journal of Political Economy* 84 (1976): 1161–76.

———. "Flexible Exchange Rates for Capital Mobility." *Brookings Papers on Economic Activity* 1 (1986): 209–26.

———. "Debt Problems and the World Macroeconomy." In *Developing Country Debt and Economic Performance: The International Financial System*, Vol. 1, edited by Jeffrey Sachs. Chicago: University of Chicago Press, 1989.

Eaton, Jonathan, and Mark Gersovitz. *Poor Country Borrowing in Private Financial Markets and the Repudiation Issue*. Princeton Studies in International Finance, no. 47. Princeton University, Department of Economics, International Finance Section, 1981.

Economist. "Unsettling." 7 May 1994.

———. "Rational Economic Man: The Titman Factor." 24 December 1994.

Eggertsson, Thráinn. *Economic Behavior and Institutions*. Cambridge Surveys of Economic Literature. New York: Cambridge University Press, 1990.

Eichengreen, Barry, and Charles Wyplosz. "The Unstable EMS." *Brookings Papers on Economic Activity* 1 (1993): 51–124.

Eichengreen, Barry, James Tobin, and Charles Wyplosz. "Two Cases for Sand in the Wheels of International Finance." *Economic Journal* 105 (1995): 162–72.

Eucken, Walter. *Die Grundsteine der Nationalökonomie* [1939]. 5th rev. ed. Godesberg: Küpper, 1947.

———. *Grundsätze der Wirtschaftspolitik* [1952]. 6th ed. Tübingen: J. C. B. Mohr, 1990.

Fingleton, John, ed. *The Internationalisation of Capital Markets and the Regulatory Response*. London: Graham and Trotman, 1992.

Fisher, Irvin. *Booms and Depressions*. New York: Adelphi, 1932.

———. "The Debt Deflation Theory of Great Depressions." *Econometrica* 1 (1933): 337–57.

Flanders, Stephanie. "History Lessons." *Financial Times*. 19 June 1995.

Frieden, Jeffry. *Banking on the World: The Politics of American International Finance*. New York: Harper and Row, 1987.

Friedman, Milton, and Anna Schwartz. *A Monetary History of the United States*. Princeton: Princeton University Press, 1963.

Gauthier, David. *Morals by Agreement*. Oxford: Clarendon, 1985.

Gibson, Heather. *The Eurocurrency Markets, Domestic Financial Policy and International Instability*. New York: St. Martin's, 1989.

Gilbert, R. Alton. "Implications of Netting Arrangements for Bank Risk in Foreign Exchange Transactions." *The Federal Reserve Bank of St. Louis Review* 74, no. 1 (1992): 3–16.

Gilpin, Robert. *The Political Economy of International Relations*. Princeton: Princeton University Press, 1987.

———. "Where Does Japan Fit In?" In *The International Relations of Japan*, edited by Kathleen Newland. London: Macmillan, 1990.

Goodhart, Charles. *The Evolution of Central Banks*. Cambridge, Mass.: MIT, 1988.

Groom, A. J. R., and Alexis Heraclides. "Integration and Disintegration." In *International Relations: A Handbook of Current Theory*, edited by Margot Light and A. J. R. Groom. London: Pinter, 1985.

Group of Thirty. Conference on Clearance and Settlement Systems, London, 14 February 1990: Speeches. London: Group of Thirty, 1990.

Guttentag, Jack, and Richard Herring. *The Lender of Last Resort Function in an International Context*. Princeton Essays in International Finance, no. 151. Princeton University, Department of Economics, International Finance Section, 1983.

Haas, Ernst. *The Uniting of Europe: Political, Social and Economic Forces*. London: Stevens, 1958.

———. *Beyond the Nation State*. Stanford: Stanford University Press, 1964.

Haas, Peter. 1992a. "Introduction: Epistemic Communities and International Policy Coordination." *International Organization* 46, no. 1: 1–35.

———. 1992b. "Obtaining International Environmental Protection through Epistemic Consensus." In *Global Environmental Change and International Relations*, edited by Ian Rowlands and Malory Greene. London: Macmillan and Millennium.

Haggard, Stephan, and Beth Simmons. "Theories of International Regimes." *International Organization* 41, no. 3 (1987): 491–517.

Hartmann, Wendelin. "A Central Banker's Perspective on International Netting and Settlement Arrangements." *Payment Systems Worldwide* (Summer 1991): 34–38.

Hayek, Friedrich von. *The Road to Serfdom* [1944]. London: Routledge, 1991.

———. *New Studies in Philosophy, Politics, and the History of Ideas*. London: Routledge and Kegan Paul, 1978.

———. "Evolution und Spontane Ordnung." Public lecture held at Bank Hofmann on 5 July 1983 in Zürich.

Helleiner, Eric. "The Internationalization of Private Finance and the Changing Postwar Order: The Unplanned Child." Paper prepared for the International Studies Association/British International Studies Association Conference in London, 28 March–1 April 1989.

———. "States and the Future of Global Finance." *Review of International Studies* 18 (1992): 31–49.

———. *States and the Reemergence of Global Finance: From Bretton Woods to the 1990s*. Ithaca: Cornell University Press, 1994.

Herring, Richard, and Robert Litan. *Financial Regulation in the Global Economy*. Washington, D.C.: Brookings Institution, 1995.

Hobbes, Thomas. *Leviathan* [1651]. Edited by Richard Tuck. Cambridge: Cambridge University Press, 1991.

Holsti, Ole. *Crisis Escalation War*. Montreal: McGill University Press, 1970.

Horsefield, J. Keith, ed. *The International Monetary Fund, 1945–1965: Twenty Years of International Monetary Cooperation*, Vol. 3, *Documents*. Washington, D.C.: International Monetary Fund, 1969.

Huertas, Thomas. "US Multinational Banking: History and Prospects." In *Banks as Multinationals*, edited by Geoffrey Jones. London: Routledge, 1990.

IBCA. "The Mexican Crisis: IBCA Sovereign Comment." 30 December 1994.

International Currency Review. "The Worrying Costs of Deregulation." 21, no. 4 (1992): 15–16.

International Finance Corporation. *Emerging Stock Markets Factbook 1994*. Washington, D.C.: International Finance Corporation, 1995.

International Monetary Fund Survey. "Commercial Bank Debt-Restructuring: The Bulgarian Experience." 17 July 1995.

Jasay, Anthony De. *Social Contract, Free Ride: A Study of the Public Goods Problem*. Oxford: Clarendon, 1989.

Jensen, Michael, and William Meckling. "Theory of the Firm: Managerial Behavior, Agency Costs, and Ownership Structure." *Journal of Financial Economics* 3, no. 4 (1976): 305–60.

Jervis, Robert. *Perception and Misperception in International Politics*. Princeton: Princeton University Press, 1976.

Kant, Immanuel. "Idee zu einer allgemeinen Geschichte in weltbürgerlicher Absicht" [1784]. In *Kleinere Schriften zur Geschichtsphilosophie Ethik und Politik*, edited by Karl Vorländer. Hamburg: Felix Meiner Verlag, 1973.

———. "Zum Ewigen Frieden: Ein philosophischer Entwurf" [1795]. In *Kleinere Schriften zur Geschichtsphilosophie Ethik und Politik*, edited by Karl Vorländer. Hamburg: Felix Meiner Verlag, 1973.

Kapstein, Ethan. "Resolving the Regulator's Dilemma: International Coordination of Banking Regulations." *International Organization* 43, no. 2 (1989): 323–47.

———. *Supervising International Banks: Origins and Implications of the Basle Accord*. Princeton Essays in International Finance, no. 185. Princeton University, Department of Economics, International Finance Section, 1991.

———. "Between Power and Purpose: Central Bankers and the Politics of Regulatory Convergence." *International Organization* 46, no. 1 (1992): 265–87.

Kegley, Charles, and Eugene Wittkopf. *World Politics: Trend and Transformation*. 3rd ed. New York: St. Martin's, 1989.

Keohane, Robert. "Theory of World Politics: Structural Realism and Beyond." In *Political Science: The State of the Discipline*, edited by Ada Finifter. Washington, D.C.: American Political Science Association, 1983.

———. *After Hegemony: Cooperation and Discord in the World Political Economy*. Princeton: Princeton University Press, 1984.

———. *International Institutions and State Power: Essays in International Relations Theory*. Boulder: Westview, 1989.

Keohane, Robert, and Joseph Nye, eds. *Transnational Relations and World Politics*. London: Harvard University Press, 1973.

———. *Power and Interdependence: World Politics in Transition* [1977]. 2nd ed. Boston: Scott, Foresman, 1989.

Kindleberger, Charles. *Manias, Panics, and Crashes: A History of Financial Crises*. New York: Basic Books, 1978.

Kindleberger, Charles, and Jean-Pierre Laffargue, eds. *Financial Crises: Theory, History, and Policy*. Cambridge: Maison des Sciences de l'Homme and Cambridge University Press, 1982.

Köhler, Claus. "National Monetary Policy in an Open World Economy." In *Monetary Policy and Financial Innovations in Five Industrial Countries: The UK, the USA, West Germany, France and Japan*, edited by Stephen Frowen and Dietmar Kath. London: Macmillan, 1992.

Kraft, Joseph. *The Mexican Rescue*. New York: Group of Thirty, 1984.

Krasner, Stephen. "Structural Causes and Regime Consequences: Regimes as Intervening Variables." In *International Regimes*, edited by Stephen Krasner. Ithaca: Cornell University Press, 1983.

Kratochwil, Friedrich. *Rules, Norms, and Decisions: On the Conditions of Practical and Legal Reasoning in International Relations and Domestic Affairs*. Cambridge Studies in International Relations, no. 2. Cambridge: Cambridge University Press, 1991.

Kratochwil, Friedrich, and John Ruggie. "International Organization: A State of the Art on an Art of the State." *International Organization* 40, no. 4 (1986): 753–75.

Lakatos, Imre. *Collected Papers*. Vol. 1. Cambridge: Cambridge University Press, 1980.

Lin, Antsong, and Peggy Swanson. "Measuring Global Money Market Interrelationships: An Investigation of Five Major World Currencies." *Journal of Banking and Finance* 17 (1993): 609–28.

Lindner, Deborah. "Foreign Exchange Policy, Monetary Policy, and Capital Market Liberalization in Korea." *International Finance Discussion Papers*, no. 435. Washington, D.C.: Board of Governors of the Federal Reserve System, 1992.

Lipsey, Robert. *Introduction to Positive Economics*. London: Harper and Row, 1963.

Lipson, Charles. "Bankers' Dilemmas: Private Cooperation in Rescheduling Sovereign Debts." *World Politics: A Quarterly Journal of International Relations* 38, no. 1 (1985): 200–225).

Lissakers, Karin. "Bank Regulation and International Debt" In *Uncertain Future: Commercial Banks and the Third World*, edited by Richard Feinberg and Valeriana Kallab. Washington, D.C.: Overseas Development Council, 1984.

Locke, John. *Zwei Abhandlungen über die Regierung (Two Treatises of Government)* [1689]. Edited by Walter Euchner. Translated by Hans Jörg Hoffman. 4th ed. Frankfurt: Suhrkamp, 1989.

Lucatelli, Adriano. "Liberalismus und die internationalen Beziehungen." *Reflexion* 33 (1994): 55–57.

Mayer, Colin. "The Assessment–Financial Innovation: Curse or Blessing?" *Oxford Review of Economic Policy* 2, no. 4 (1986): i–xix.

Mendelsohn, M. S. *Commercial Banks and the Restructuring of Cross-border Debt*. New York: Group of Thirty, 1983.

Menger, Carl. *Investigations into the Method of the Social Sciences with Special Reference to Economics* [1883]. New York: New York University Press, 1985.

Minsky, Hyman. "Financial Stability Revisited: The Economics of Disaster." In *Reappraisal of the Federal Reserve Discount Mechanism*, edited by Board of Governors of the Federal Reserve System. Washington, D.C.: Federal Reserve, 1972.

—————. "The Financial-Instability Hypothesis: Capitalist Processes and the Behavior of the Economy." In *Financial Crises: Theory, History, and Policy*, edited by Charles Kindleberger and Jean-Pierre Laffargue. Cambridge: Maison des Sciences de l'Homme and Cambridge University Press, 1982.

Mises, Ludwig von. *Human Action: A Treatise on Economics*. London: William Hodge, 1949.

Moody's. *Consistency, Reliability, Integrity*. New York: Moody's, 1991.

Morgenthau, Hans. *Politics among Nations: The Struggle for Power and Peace*. 5th ed. New York: Knopf, 1973.

Neue Zürcher Zeitung. "Gefährdung der Kapitalmärkte durch Protektionismus: Hohe Liquidität als Stütze des Kursniveaus." 15 November 1993.

—————. "Plädoyer Greenspans für Selbstkontrolle der Märkte: Risiko-Management im Geschäft mit derivativen Instrumenten." 9 June 1994.

Ohmae, Kenichi. *The Borderless World: Power and Strategy in the Interlinked Economy*. London: Fontana, 1992.

Padoa-Schioppa, Tommaso, and Fabrizio Saccomanni. "Managing a Market-Led Global Financial System." In *Managing the World Economy: Fifty Years after Bretton Woods*, edited by Peter Kenen. Washington, D.C.: Institute for International Economics, 1994.

Pagano, Marco. "Financial Markets and Growth." *European Economic Review* (1993): 613–22.

Panic, Milivoje. *National Management of the International Economy*. London: Macmillan, 1988.

Pauly, Louis. *Opening Financial Markets: Banking Politics on the Pacific Rim*. Ithaca: Cornell University Press, 1988.

Pecchioli, Rinaldo. *The Internationalisation of Banking*. Paris: Organization for Economic Cooperation and Development, 1983.

—————. *Prudential Supervision in Banking*. Paris: Organization for Economic Cooperation and Development, 1987.

Polanyi, Karl. *The Great Transformation: Politische und ökonomische Ursprünge von Gesellschaften und Wirtschaftssystemen* [1944]. Translated by Heinrich Jelinek. 2nd ed. Frankfurt: Suhrkamp, 1990.

Popper, Karl. *Logik der Forschung* [1935]. 9th ed. Tübingen: J. C. B. Mohr, 1989.

Portes, Richard, and Alexander Swoboda, eds. *Threats to International Financial Stability*. Cambridge: Cambridge University Press, 1987.

Robinson, Joan. *The Rate of Interest and Other Essays*. London: Macmillan, 1952.

Rosenberg, Justin. "The International Imagination: IR Theory and 'Classic Social Analysis.' " *Millennium: Journal of International Studies* 23, no. 1 (1994): 85–108.

Rudloff, Hans-Jörg. "The Role of International Capital Markets in a Changing World." *Euromoney* (September 1993): 193–94.

Ruggie, John. "International Responses to Technology." *International Organization* 29, no. 3 (1975): 557–84.

Ruloff, Dieter. *Weltstaat oder Staatenwelt: Über die Chancen globaler Zusammenarbeit*. München: Beck, 1988.

Sachs, Jeffrey. *Theoretical Issues in International Borrowing*. Princeton Essays in International Finance, no. 54. Princeton University, Department of Economics, International Finance Section, 1984.

98 References

————. "Managing the LDC Debt Crisis." *Brookings Papers on Economic Activity*, no. 2. Washington, D.C.: Brookings Institution, 1986.

Sakakibara, Eisuke. "The Japanese Financial System in Transition." In *The Future of the International Monetary System*, edited by Tamir Agmon et al. Lexington: Lexington Books, 1984.

Sarver, Eugene. *Eurocurrency Market Handbook*. 2nd ed. New York: New York Institute of Finance, 1990.

Schwartz, Anna. "Real and Pseudo-Financial Crises." In *Financial Crises and the World Banking System*, edited by Forrest Capie and Geoffrey Wood. New York: St. Martin's, 1986.

Seldon, Arthur, ed. *Financial Regulation—Or Over-Regulation?* London: Institute of Economic Affairs, 1988.

Shirreff, David. "Can Anyone Tame the Currency Market?" *Euromoney* (September 1993): 60–69.

Smith, Adam. *Der Wohlstand der Nationen: Eine Untersuchung seiner Natur und seiner Ursachen* [1776]. Translated by Horst Claus Recktenwald. 6th ed. München: Deutscher Taschenbuch Verlag, 1993.

Spero, Joan E. *The Failure of the Franklin National Bank: Challenge to the International Banking System*. New York: Columbia University Press, 1980.

————. *The Politics of International Economic Relations*. 4th ed. New York: St. Martin's, 1990.

Staley, Charles. *A History of Economic Thought: From Aristotle to Arrow*. Cambridge, Mass.: Basil Blackwell, 1991.

Staniland, Martin. *What Is Political Economy? A Study of Social Theory and Underdevelopment*. New Haven: Yale University Press, 1985.

Strange, Susan. *Casino Capitalism*. Oxford: Blackwell, 1986.

————. *States and Markets: An Introduction to International Political Economy*. London: Pinter, 1989.

Swoboda, Alexander. "Debt and the Efficiency and Stability of the International Financial System." In *International Debt and the Developing Countries*, edited by Gordon Smith and John Cuddington. Washington, D.C.: The World Bank, 1985.

Takeda, Masahiko, and Philip Turner. *The Liberalisation of Japan's Financial Markets: Some Major Themes*. Bank for International Settlements Economic Paper, no. 34. Basle: Bank for International Settlements, November 1992.

Tavlas, George, and Yuzuru Ozeki. "The Internationalization of the Yen." *Finance and Development* (June 1991): 2–5.

————. "The Internationalization of Currencies: An Appraisal of the Japanese Yen." *International Monetary Fund Occasional Paper*, no. 90. Washington, D.C.: International Monetary Fund, January 1992.

Thornton, Henry. *An Enquiry into the Nature and Effects of the Paper Credit of Great Britain* [1802]. New York: Rinehart, 1939.

Tobin, James. "A Proposal for International Monetary Reform." *Eastern Economic Journal* 4, nos. 3–4 (1978): 153–59.

Underhill, Geoffrey. "Markets beyond Politics? The State and the Internationalization of Financial Markets." *European Journal of Political Research* 19 (1991): 197–225.

———. "Keeping Governments out of Politics: Transnational Securities Markets, Regulatory Cooperation, and Political Legitimacy." Unpublished paper, University of Warwick, March 1993.

Varnholt, Burkhard. *Systemrisiken auf Finanzmärkten unter besonderer Berücksichtigung der Märkte für Derivate*. Bern: Haupt, 1995.

Walter, Andrew. *World Power and World Money: The Role of Hegemony and International Monetary Order*. London: Harvester Wheatsheaf, 1993.

Wendt, Alexander. "Anarchy Is What States Make of It: The Social Construction of Power Politics." *International Organization* 46, no. 2 (1992): 391–425.

Yarbrough, Beth, and Robert Yarbrough. "International Institutions and the New Economics of Organization." *International Organization* 44, no. 2 (1990): 235–59.

Zobl, Dieter, and Thomas Werlen. *Die Rechtsprobleme des bilateralen Netting*. Zürich: Schulthess Polygraphischer Verlag, 1994.

Further Reading

Andermatt, Richard. "Vom Troubleshooter zum internationalen Finanzforum." *SKA Bulletin*. September/October 1995.

Arrow, Kenneth. *The Limits of Organization*. New York: W.W. Norton, 1974.

Artis, Michael, and Silvia Ostry. *International Economic Policy Coordination*. Chatham House Papers, no. 30. Royal Institute of International Affairs. London: Routledge, 1986.

Aschinger, Gerhard. "The Nature of Financial Crises." *Prospects* 3 (July/August 1996).

Bair, Sheila. "Clearing House Issues in OTC Derivatives Markets." *World of Banking*. May/June 1994.

Baltensperger, Ernst. "Alternative Approaches to the Theory of the Banking Firm." *Journal of Monetary Economics* 4 (1980): 1–37.

Bank for International Settlements. *Public Disclosure of Market and Credit Risks by Financial Intermediaries*. Basle: Bank for International Settlements, 1994.

————. *Macroeconomic and Monetary Policy Issues Raised by the Growth of Derivatives Markets*. Basle: Bank for International Settlements, 1994.

————. *Prudential Supervision of Banks' Derivatives Activities*. Basle: Bank for International Settlements, 1994.

————. *Settlement Risk in Foreign Exchange Transactions*. Basle: Bank for International Settlements, 1996.

Banks, Michael. "The Inter-Paradigm Debate." In *International Relations: A Handbook of Current Theory*, edited by Margot Light and A. J. R. Groom. London: Pinter, 1985.

Barro, Robert. "Latin Lessons in Monetary Policy." *Wall Street Journal Europe*. 2 May 1995.

Beitz, Charles. *Political Theory and International Relations*. Princeton: Princeton University Press, 1979.

Benzie, Richard. *The Development of the International Bond Market*. Bank for International Settlements Economic Paper, no. 32. Basle: Bank for International Settlements, 1992.

Bernauer, Thomas. "Der Staat ist tot! Es lebe der Staat! Globalisierungsprozesse und Grundstrukturen des internationalen Systems." *Schweizer Monatshefte*, Vol. 76, no. 11 (1996): 30–33.

Bernstein, Peter. *Against the Gods: The Remarkable Story of Risk.* Chichester: Wiley, 1996.

Blower, Bob. "The Use of Netting in Foreign Exchange Settlement." *World of Banking.* January/February 1995.

Bordo, Michael. "Braucht die Welt ein neues 'Bretton Woods'?: Ein wirtschaftshistorischer Rückblick auf alternative Währungsordnungen." *Neue Zürcher Zeitung.* 25–26 March 1995.

Brainard, Lawrence. "More Lending to the Third World? A Banker's View." In *Uncertain Future: Commercial Banks and the Third World,* edited by Richard Feinberg and Valeriana Kallab. Washington, D.C.: Overseas Development Council, 1984.

Bull, Hedley. *The Anarchical Society: A Study of Order in World Politics.* London: Macmillan, 1977.

Coase, Ronald. "The Choice of Institutional Framework: A Comment." *Journal of Institutional and Theoretical Economics* 140 (1974): 493–96.

———. *The Firm, the Market, and the Law.* Chicago: University of Chicago Press, 1984.

Cohen, Benjamin. *Organizing the World's Money: The Political Economy of International Monetary Relations.* London: Macmillan, 1977.

———. "Phoenix Risen: The Resurrection of Global Finance." *World Politics* 48 (1996): 268–96.

Cohen, Bernice. *The Edge of Chaos: Financial Booms, Bubbles, Crashes and Chaos.* Chichester: Wiley, 1997.

Cooper, Richard. "Economic Interdependencies and Coordination of Policies." In *Economic Policy in an Interdependent World,* edited by Richard Cooper. Cambridge, Mass.: MIT, 1986.

Cornes, Richard, and Todd Sandler. *The Theory of Externalities, Public Goods, and Club Goods.* Cambridge: Cambridge University Press, 1986.

Dale, Richard. *International Banking Deregulation: The Great Banking Experiment.* Oxford: Blackwell, 1992.

Dowd, Kevin. *Laissez-faire Banking.* London: Routledge, 1993.

Economist. "The Collapse of Barings: A Fallen Star." 4 March 1995.

———. "Fixed and Floating Voters." 1 April 1995.

———. "The Shape of the World: The Nation-state Is Dead. Long Live the Nation-state." 23 December 1995.

Edwards, Franklin, and Frederic Mishkin. *The Decline of Traditional Banking: Implications for Financial Stability and Regulatory Policy.* Working Paper no. 4993. National Bureau of Economic Research. January 1995.

Feldstein, Martin. "Global Capital Flows: Too Little, Not Too Much." *Economist.* 24 June 1995.

Fischer, Stanley. "International Capital Flows, the International Agencies and Financial Stability." *MIT Industrial Liaison Program Report.* 26 June 1994.

Fischer-Erlach, Peter. *Handel und Kursbildung am Devisenmarkt.* 2nd ed. Stuttgart: Kohlhammer, 1985.

Fox, Gerald. "An Update on Automated Clearing Houses in the U.S." *World of Banking.* May/June 1993.

Frankfurter Allgemeine Zeitung. "Die Devisensteuer findet immer mehr Freunde: Untaugliches Mittel gegen kurzfristige Kursbewegungen der Währungen." 17 March 1995.

Frei, Christoph, and Robert Nef, eds. *Contending with Hayek: On Liberalism, Spontaneous Order and the Post-Communist Societies in Transition.* Bern: Lang, 1994.

Frey, Bruno. *Internationale Politische Ökonomie.* München: Verlag Vahlen, 1985.

Glen, Jack, and Brian Pinto. "Kapitalmärkte und Unternehmen in Entwicklungsländern." *Finanzierung und Entwicklung.* March 1995.

Goldsmith, Raymond. "Comment on Hyman Minsky: The Financial Instability Hypothesis." In *Financial Crises: Theory, History, and Policy,* edited by Charles Kindleberger and Jean-Pierre Laffargue. Cambridge: Maison des Sciences de l'Hommes and Cambridge University Press, 1982.

Goldthorpe, John, ed. *Order and Conflict in Contemporary Capitalism.* Oxford: Clarendon, 1984.

Goodman, John. *Monetary Sovereignty: The Politics of Central Banking in Western Europe.* Ithaca: Cornell University Press, 1992.

Goodman, John, and Louis Pauly. "The Obsolescence of Capital Controls? Economic Management in an Age of Global Markets." *World Politics* 46, no. 1 (1993): 50–82.

Greenslade, Jenni. "Real Exchange Rates: What Can They Tell Us?" *Economic Outlook.* Center for Economic Forecasting, London Business School, February 1995.

Grieco, Joseph. "Anarchy and the Limits of Cooperation: A Realist Critique of the Newest Liberal Institutionalism." *International Organization* 42, no. 3 (1988): 485–507.

Groom, A. J. R., and Paul Taylor, eds. *Framework for International Co-operation.* London: Pinter, 1990.

Group of Thirty. *The Foreign Exchange Markets under Floating Rates.* New York: Group of Thirty, 1980.

Haindl, Andreas. *The Euro Money Market: A Strategic Analysis of Bank Operations.* Bern: Haupt, 1991.

Hankel, Wilhelm. "Eine neue Leitwährung wird gesucht: Währungswettbewerb versagt als weltwirtschaftliches Ordnungsprinzip." *Handelsblatt.* 26 April 1995.

———. *Das grosse Geld-Theater: Über DM, Dollar, Rubel und Ecu.* Stuttgart: Deutsche Verlags-Anstalt, 1995.

Hayek, Friedrich von. *Individualism and Economic Order.* Chicago: University of Chicago Press, 1948.

———. *The Fatal Conceit: The Errors of Socialism.* Chicago: University of Chicago Press, 1988.

Horne, Jocelyn, and Paul Masson. *Scope and Limits of International Economic Cooperation and Policy Coordination.* International Monetary Fund Staff Paper (1988): 259–96.

Kapstein, Ethan. *Governing the Global Economy: International Finance and the State.* Cambridge: Harvard University Press, 1994.

Kenen, Peter. *Managing Exchange Rates.* London: Routledge and the Royal Institute of International Affairs, 1988.

Khademian, Anne. *Checking on Banks: Autonomy and Accountability in Three Federal Agencies.* Washington, D.C.: Brookings Institution, 1996.

Kiehling, Hartmut. "Das Chaos an den Finanzmärkten." *Schweizer Bank.* May 1995.

Kindleberger, Charles. *Power and Money: The Economics of International Politics and the Politics of International Economics.* New York: Basic Books, 1970.

Knabenhans, Walter. "Selbstregulierung oder Staatsaufsicht? Derivate im Visier der Aufsichtsbehörden." *SKA Bulletin*. May/June 1995.

Knorr, Klaus. *Power and Wealth: The Political Economy of International Power*. London: Macmillan, 1973.

Koslowski, Peter. *Die Ordnung der Wirtschaft*. Studien zur praktischen Philosophie und Politischen Ökonomie. Tübingen: J. C. B. Mohr, 1994.

Kulessa, Margareta. "The Tobin Tax: A Tool for Allocative or Distributional Policies?" *Intereconomics*. May/June 1996.

Lastra, Rosa Maria. *Central Banking and Banking Regulation*. London: London School of Economics, 1996.

Linklater, Andrew. *Beyond Realism and Marxism: Critical Theory and International Relations*. London: Macmillan, 1990.

———. *Men and Citizens in the Theory of International Relations*. 2nd ed. London: Macmillan and London School of Economics and Political Science, 1990.

Litan, Robert. *What Should Banks Do?* Washington, D.C.: Brookings Institution, 1987.

Lucatelli, Adriano. "Amnesty International: Politischer Idealismus versus Politischen Realismus." *Schweizer Monatshefte*. Vol. 73, no. 4 (1993): 277–280.

Lucatelli, Adriano, and Claudia Jäggi. "Der Devisenhandel ist tot - es lebe der Devisenhandel: Rückgang des Marktvolumens um einen Fünftel." *Neue Zürcher Zeitung*. 18 February 1997.

Maki, Uskali, Bo Gustaffsson, and Christian Knudsen, eds. *Rationality, Institutions and Economic Methodology*. London: Routledge, 1994.

Mankiw, N. Gregory. "The Allocation of Credit and Financial Collapse." *Quarterly Journal of Economics* 101 (1987): 455–70.

Millman, Gregory. *The Vandels' Crown: How Rebel Currency Traders Overthrew the World's Central Banks*. New York: Free Press, 1995.

———. "Barings Collapses; Financial System Bears Up Well." *Wall Street Journal Europe*. 1 March 1995.

Mitrany, David. *A Working Peace System*. Chicago: Quadrangle Books, 1966.

———. *The Functional Theory of Politics*. London: London School of Economics and Political Science and Martin Robertson, 1975.

Moe, Terry. "The New Economics of Organization." *American Journal of Political Science* 28 (1984): 739–77.

Moïsi, Dominique. "Citizens on a Sinking Ship." *Financial Times*. 26 July 1996.

Moody's. *Moody's Rating Process: Introduction*. New York: Moody's, 1989.

Moran, Michael. *The Politics of the Financial Services Revolution*. London: Macmillan, 1991.

Morse, Edward. *Modernization and the Transformation of International Relations*. New York: Free Press, 1976.

Mueller, Dennis. *Public Choice II*. Cambridge: Cambridge University Press, 1989.

Müller, Harald. *Die Chance der Kooperation: Regime in den Internationalen Beziehungen*. Darmstadt: Wissenschaftliche Buchgesellschaft, 1993.

Neue Zürcher Zeitung. "Selbstregulierende Kräfte in der Währungskrise." 27 March 1995.

———. "Der Nationalstaat im Zeichen der Globalisierung." 10 June 1996.

Neufeld, Mark. "Reflexivity and International Relations Theory." *Millennium: Journal of International Studies* 22, no. 1. (1993): 53–76.

Nicholson, Michael. *Formal Theories of International Relations*. Cambridge: Cambridge University Press, 1990.

Niehans, Jürg. *The Theory of Money*. Baltimore: Johns Hopkins University Press, 1978.

North, Douglass. *Institutions, Institutional Change, and Economic Performance*. Cambridge: Cambridge University Press, 1990.

Nozick, Robert. *Anarchy, State, and Utopia*. New York: Basic Books, 1974.

Nye, Joseph. "Neorealism and Neoliberalism." *World Politics* 40, no. 2 (1988): 235–51.

O'Brien, Richard. "Who Rules the World's Financial Markets?" *Harvard Business Review*. March/April 1995.

Odell, John. *U.S. International Monetary Policy: Markets, Power, and Ideas as Sources of Change*. Princeton: Princeton University Press, 1982.

Olson, Mancur. *The Logic of Collective Actions: Public Goods and the Theory of Groups*. Cambridge, Mass.: Harvard University Press, 1965.

Ostrom, Elinor, James Walker, and Roy Gardner. "Covenants with and without a Sword. Self-Governance Is Possible." *American Political Science Review* 86 (1992): 404–17.

Osugi, K. *Japan's Experience of Financial Deregulation Since 1984 in an International Perspective*. Bank for International Settlements Economic Paper, no. 26. Basle: Bank for International Settlements, 1990.

Ottel, Wilfried. "Netting: Zauberwort des Risk-Managements und Element des internationalen Konkurrenzkampfes." *Schweizer Bank*. March 1995.

Oye, Kenneth, ed. *Cooperation under Anarchy*. Princeton: Princeton University Press, 1986.

———. *Economic Discrimination and Political Exchange: World Political Economy in the 1930s and 1980s*. Princeton: Princeton University Press, 1992.

Peterson, Erik. "Surrendering to Markets." *The Washington Quarterly* (Autumn 1995): 103–15.

Petzel, Todd. "Self-Regulation and Futures Markets: Benefits from Technology Gains." In *Technology and the Regulation of Financial Markets*, edited by Anthony Saunders and Lawrence White. Lexington: Lexington Books, 1986.

Popper, Karl. *The Poverty of Historicism*. London: Routledge and Kegan Paul, 1961.

Porter, Tony. *States, Markets, and Regimes in Global Finance*. New York: St. Martin's, 1993.

Portes, Richard. "Let's Fight the Next Sovereign Debt War Now." *Economic Outlook*. Center for Economic Forecasting, London Business School, February 1996.

Radzicki, Michael. "Institutional Dynamics, Deterministic Chaos, and Self-Organizing Systems." *Journal of Economic Issues* 24 (1994): 57–102.

Ramonet, Ignacio. "Formen der Macht am Ende des 20. Jahrhunderts." *Le Monde Diplomatique. Die Tageszeitung/Woz*. May 1995.

Rapoport, Anatol. *Fights, Games, Debates*. Ann Arbor: University of Michigan Press, 1960.

Reichenstein, Peter Marcus. *Währungsreserven und Reservepolitik bei flexiblen Wechselkursen*. Grüsch: Verlag Rüegger, 1987.

Rhodes, William. "Lessons Emerge from Mexican Crisis." *Financial Times*. 23 June 1995.

Richman, Louis. "Worrying about World Markets." *Fortune*. 24 July 1995.

Rosecrance, Richard. "International Theory Revisited." *International Organization* 35, no. 4 (1981): 691–713.

———. *The Rise of the Trading State: Commerce and Conquest in the Modern World*. New York: Basic Books, 1986.

Sandler, Todd. "A Theory of Intergenerational Clubs." *Economic Inquiry* 20 (1982): 191–208.

———. *Collective Action: Theory and Applications*. Ann Arbor: University of Michigan Press, 1992.

Schelling, Thomas. *The Strategy of Conflict*. New York: Oxford University Press, 1960.

Schotter, Andrew. *The Economic Theory of Social Institutions*. Cambridge: Cambridge University Press, 1981.

———. "Why Take a Game Theoretical Approach to Economics? Institutions, Economics, and Game Theory. *Economie Appliquée* 36, no. 4 (1983): 673–95.

Sened, Itai. "Contemporary Theory of Institutions in Perspective." *Journal of Theoretical Politics* 3 (1991): 379–402.

Shepsle, Kenneth. "Studying Institutions: Some Lessons from the Rational Choice Approach." *Journal of Theoretical Politics* 1 (1989): 131–47.

Shirref, David. "The Agony of the Global Supervisor." *Euromoney*. July 1996.

———. "The fear that dares to speak its name." *Euromoney*. September 1996.

Siegenthaler, Hansjörg. *Regelvertrauen, Prosperität und Krisen: Die Ungleichmässigkeiten wirtschaftlicher und sozialer Entwicklung als Ergebnis individuellen Handelns und sozialen Lernens*. Tübingen: J. C. B. Mohr, 1993.

Sirel, Florence. "Netting in Financial Markets: Broadening the Legal Perspective." *World of Banking*. March/April 1994.

Sobel, Andrew. *Domestic Choices, International Markets: Dismantling National Barriers and Liberalizing Securities Markets*. Ann Arbor: University of Michigan, 1994.

Storck, Ekkehard. *Euromarkt: Finanz-Drehscheibe der Welt*. Stuttgart: Schäffer-Poeschel Verlag, 1995.

Strebel, Brigitte. "Effizientes Netzwerk nationaler Aufsichtsbehörden." *Schweizer Bank*. May 1996.

Sugden, Robert. *The Economics of Rights, Co-operation, and Welfare*. Oxford: Blackwell, 1986.

———. "Spontaneous Order." *Journal of Economic Perspectives* 3 (1989): 85–97.

———. "Rational Choice: A Survey of Contributions from Economics and Philosophy." *Economic Journal* 101 (1991): 751–85.

Taylor, Michael. *Anarchy and Cooperation*. New York: Wiley, 1976.

———. *Community, Anarchy, and Liberty*. Cambridge: Cambridge University Press, 1982.

———. *The Possibility of Cooperation*. Cambridge: Cambridge University Press, 1987.

Telser, Lester. "A Theory of Self-Enforcing Agreements." *Journal of Business* 53 (1981): 27–44.

Tew, Brian. *The Evolution of the International Monetary System, 1945–1988*. 4th ed. London: Hutchinson, 1988.

Tyson-Davies, Richard. "World of Regulatory Compliance." *World of Banking*. January/February 1994.

Union Bank of Switzerland International Finance. "Controlling Derivative Risks." 23 (Spring 1995).

Varnholt, Burkhard. "Systemrisiken und Derivate richtig beurteilen!" *Schweizer Bank*. May 1995.

Vaubel, Roland. "A Public Choice Approach to International Organization." *Public Choice* 51 (1986): 39–57.

Vernon, Raymond. *Sovereignty at Bay: The Multinational Spread of U.S. Enterprises.* New York: Basic Books, 1971.

Walker, Rob. *Inside/Outside: International Relations as Political Theory.* Cambridge: Cambridge University Press, 1993.

Waltz, Kenneth. *Man, the State, and War: A Theoretical Analysis.* New York: Columbia University Press, 1959.

———. *Theory of International Politics.* Reading, Mass.: Addison-Wesley, 1979.

Walzer, Michael. *Spheres of Justice: A Defense of Pluralism and Equality.* New York: Basic Books, 1983.

Warde, Ibrahim. "Die Tyrannei des 'ökonomischen Korrekten.' " *Le Monde Diplomatique. Die Tageszeitung/Woz.* May 1995.

Weber, Max. *Economy and Society.* New York: Bedminster, 1968.

Williams, Howard. *International Relations in Political Theory.* Milton Keynes: Open University Press, 1992.

Williamson, Oliver. *Markets and Hierarchies: Analysis and Antitrust Implications.* New York: Free Press, 1975.

———. *The Economic Institutions of Capitalism: Firms, Markets, Relational Contracting.* New York: Free Press, 1985.

Wittmann, Walter. *Das Globale Desaster: Politik und Finanzen im Bankrott.* München: Wirtschaftsverlag Langen Müller/Herbig, 1995.

Zürn, Michael. *Interessen und Institutionen: Grundlegung und Anwendungen des situations-strukturellen Ansatzes.* Opladen: Leske und Budrich, 1992.

Index

About the Author

ADRIANO LUCATELLI is Senior Economist at Credit Suisse in Zurich. Dr. Lucatelli was formerly a foreign-exchange dealer in Zurich and Berne, and is a graduate of the London School of Economics and the University of Zurich.